04 Vienna , Paris , Aix en Provence , Rom Budapest , Lake Constance , Zurich (Black/white/ gray) Arya Bahram Art Photos Collection

عکس های هنری از آریا بهرام (مجید بهرام بیگی)

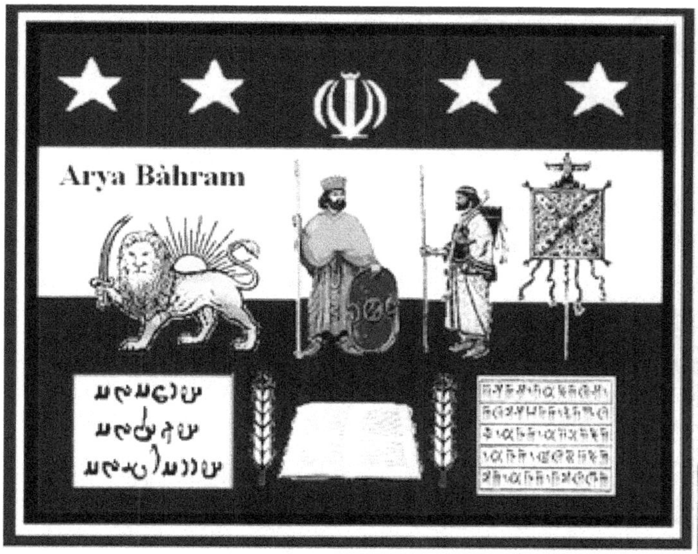

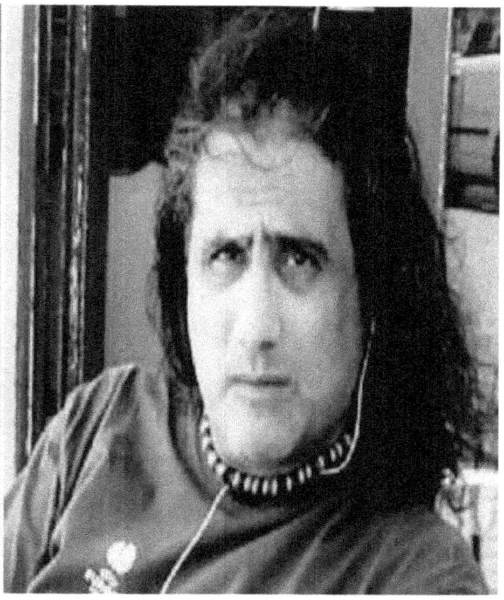

Musics for book - musiques pour livre - Musiken für Buch – آهنگها برای کتاب - Ahàng ha bàraye nibig ha

http://www.majidbahrambeiguy.at/my-foto-books---mes-livres-des-photos-.html

Arya Bàhram (Màjid Bàhram beiguy) , Österreich

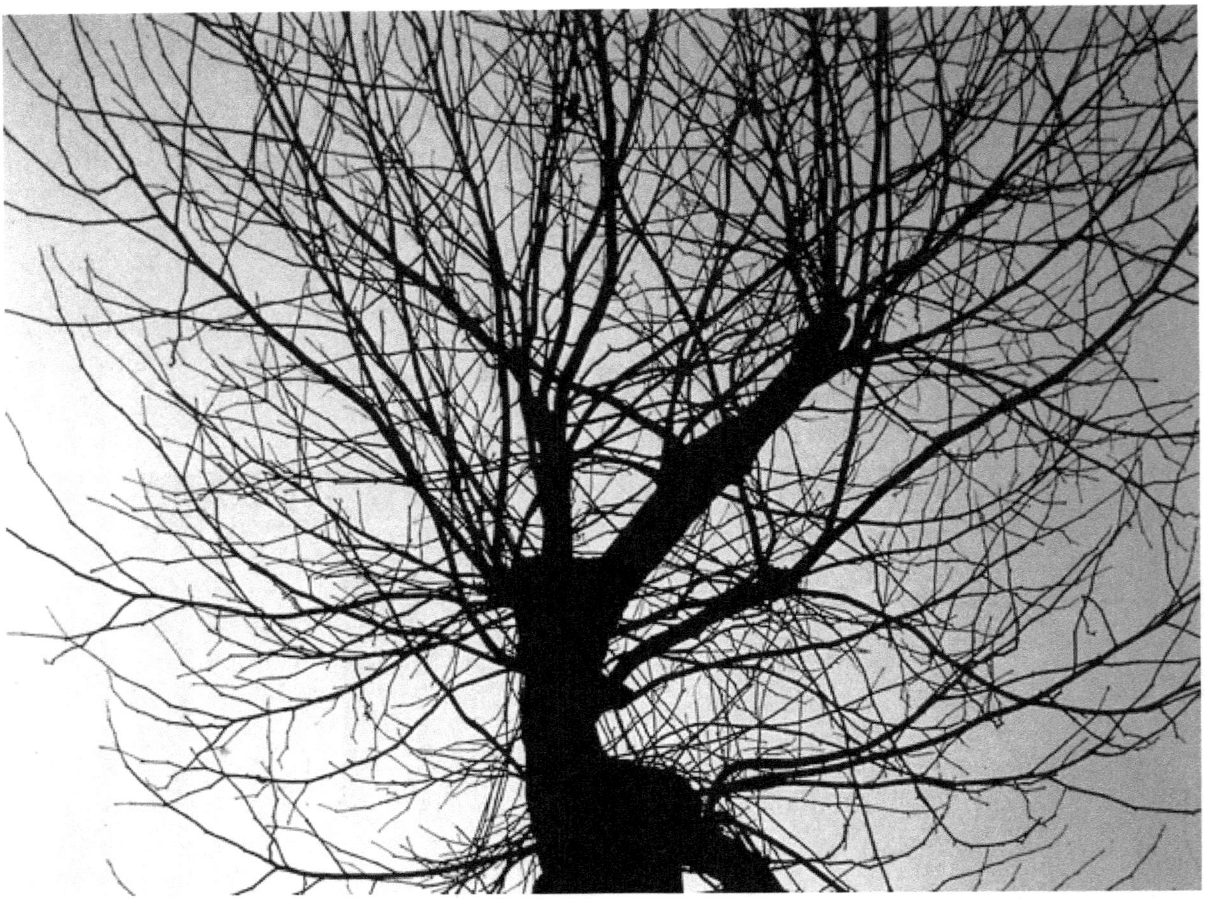

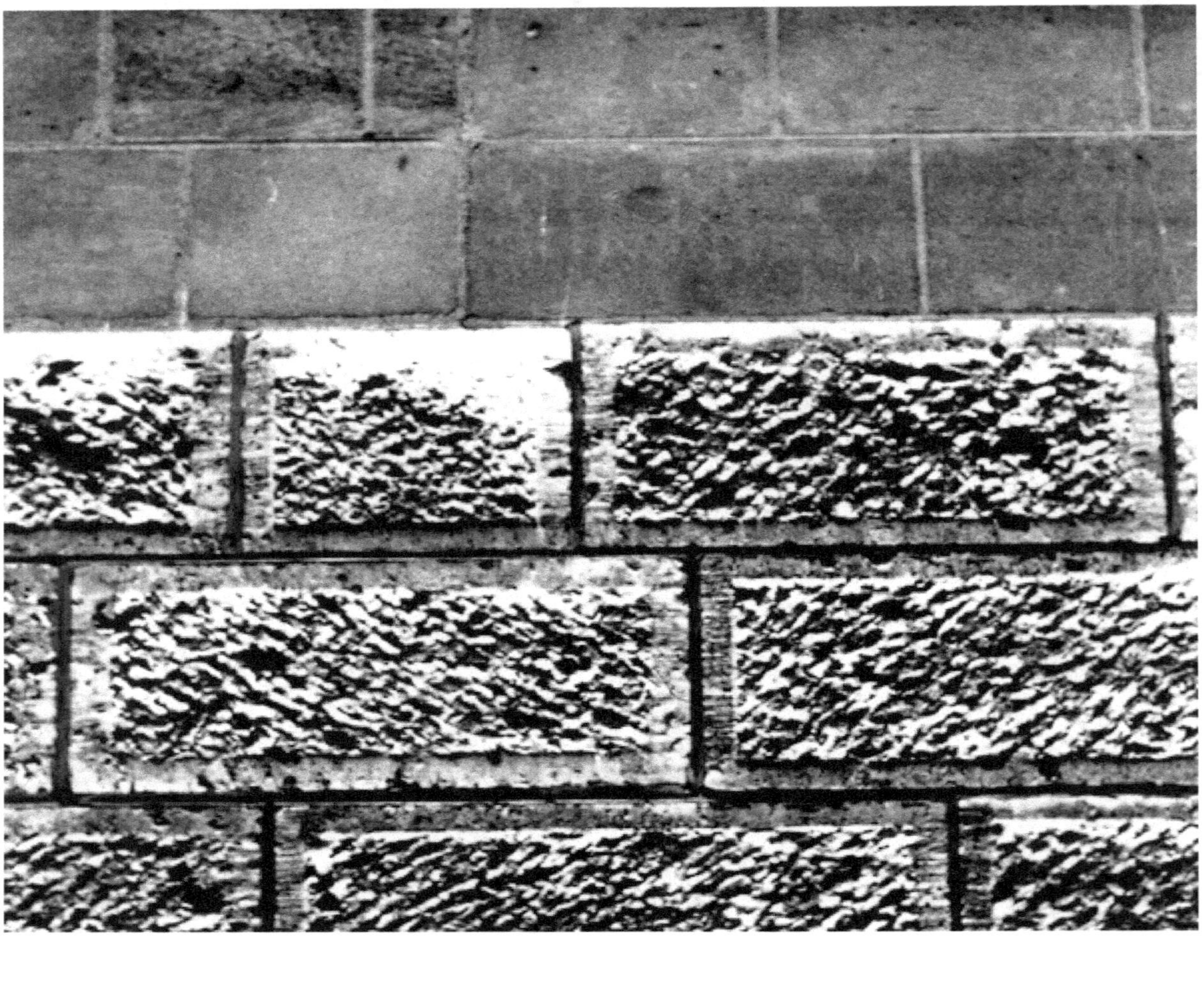

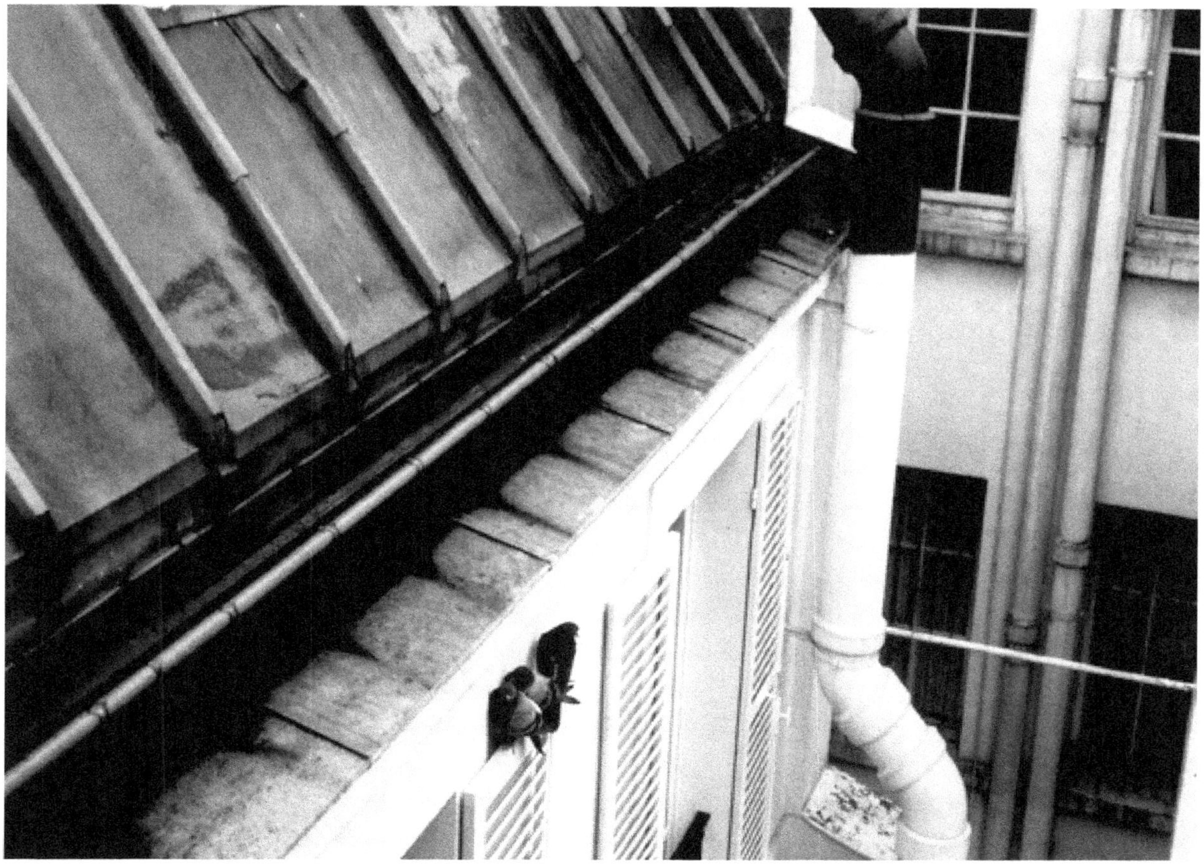

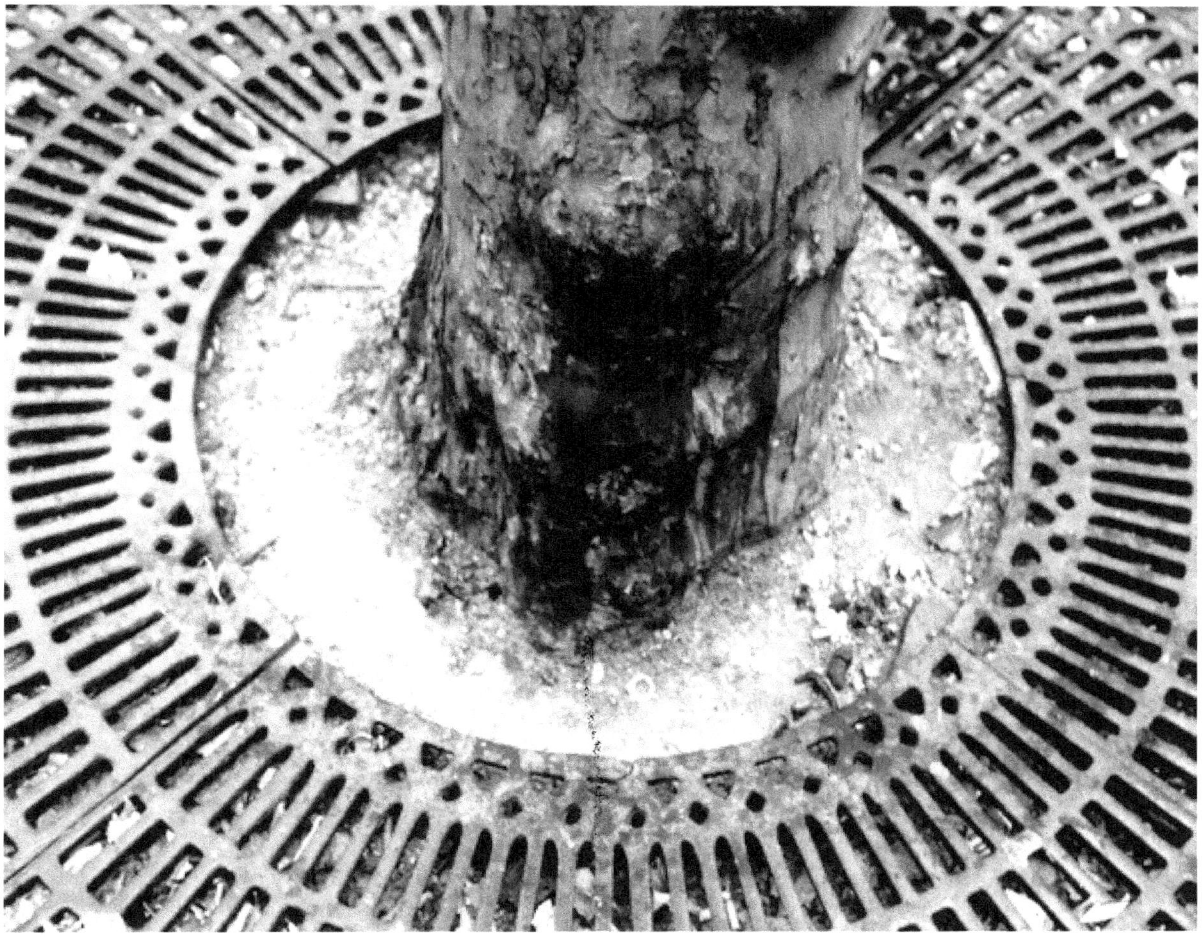

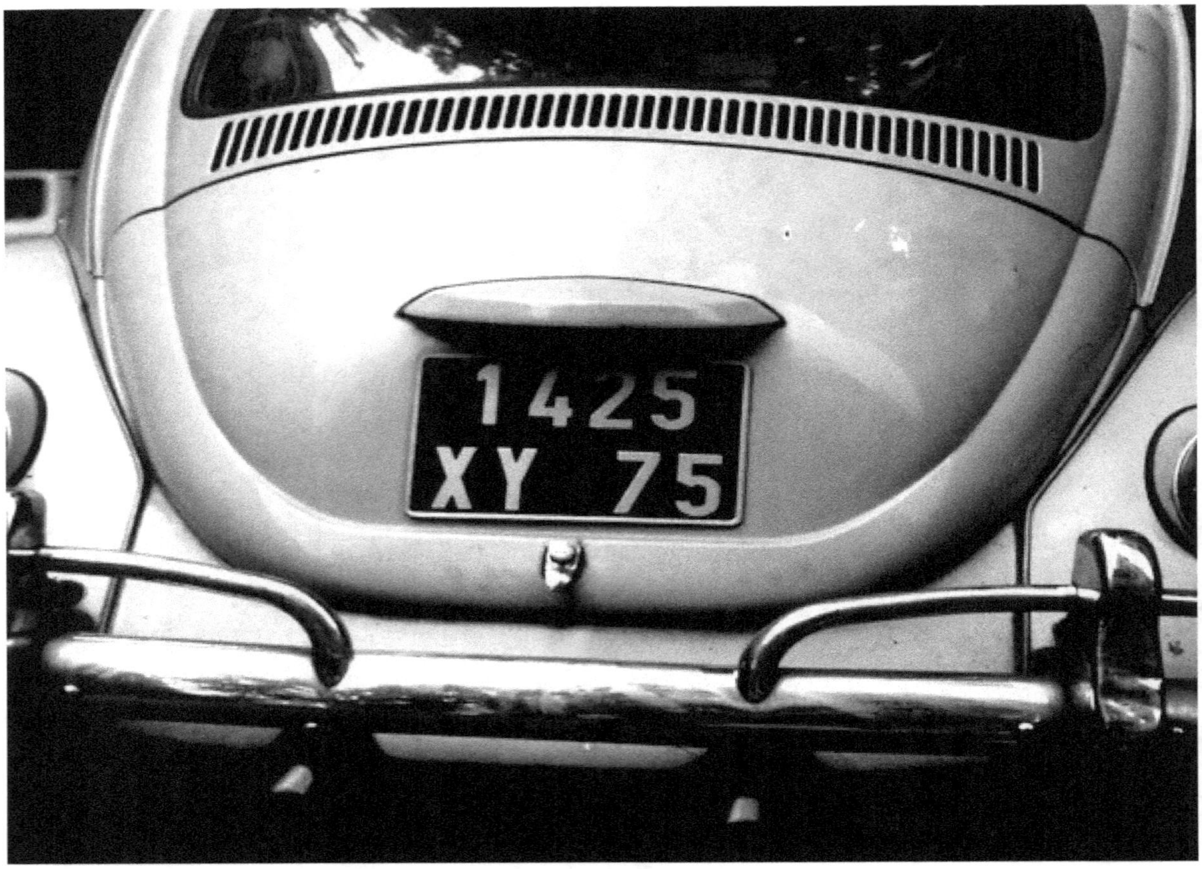
1425
XY 75

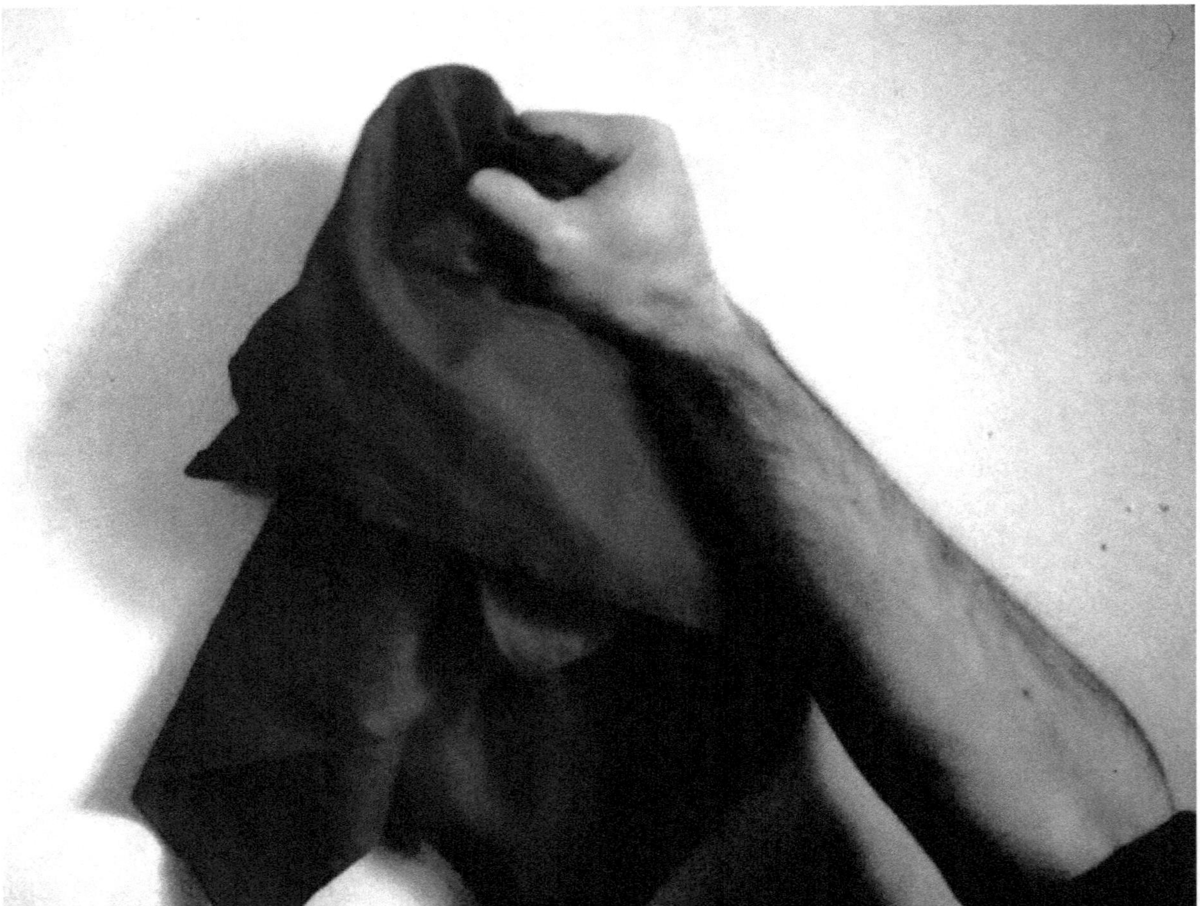

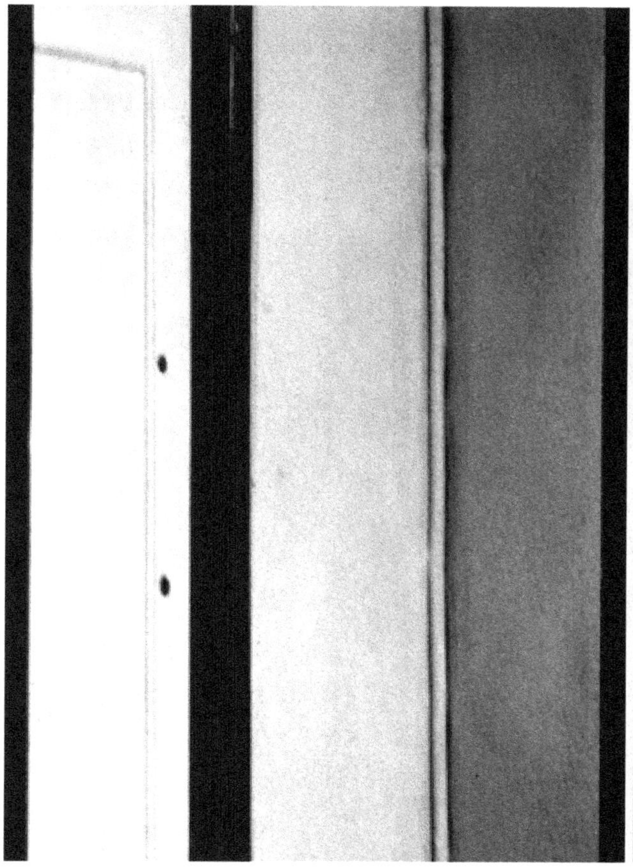

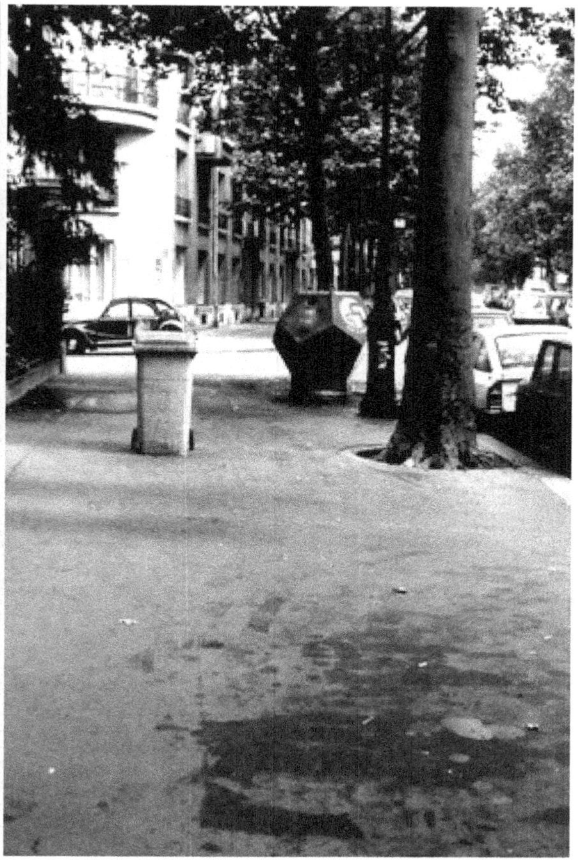

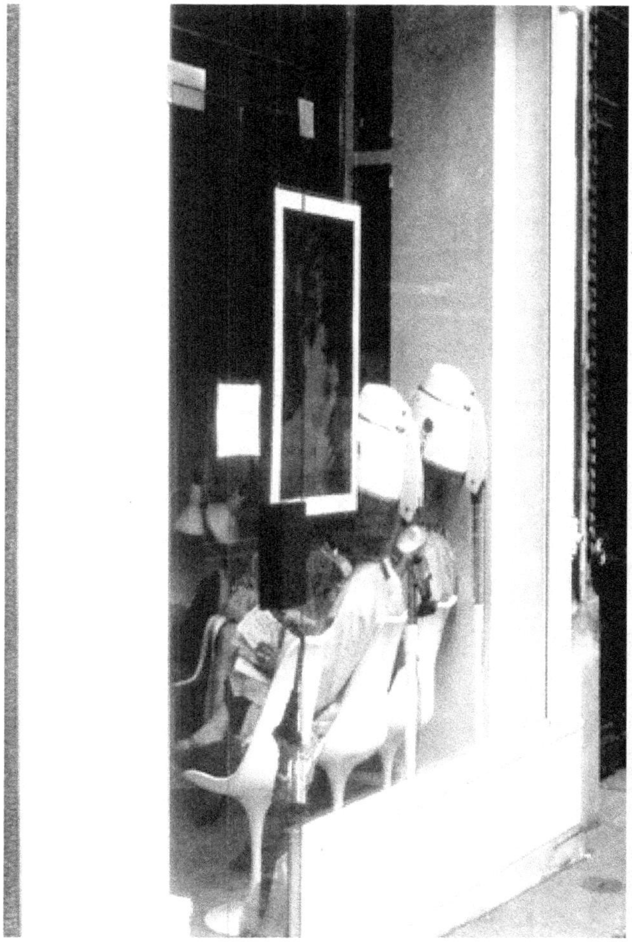

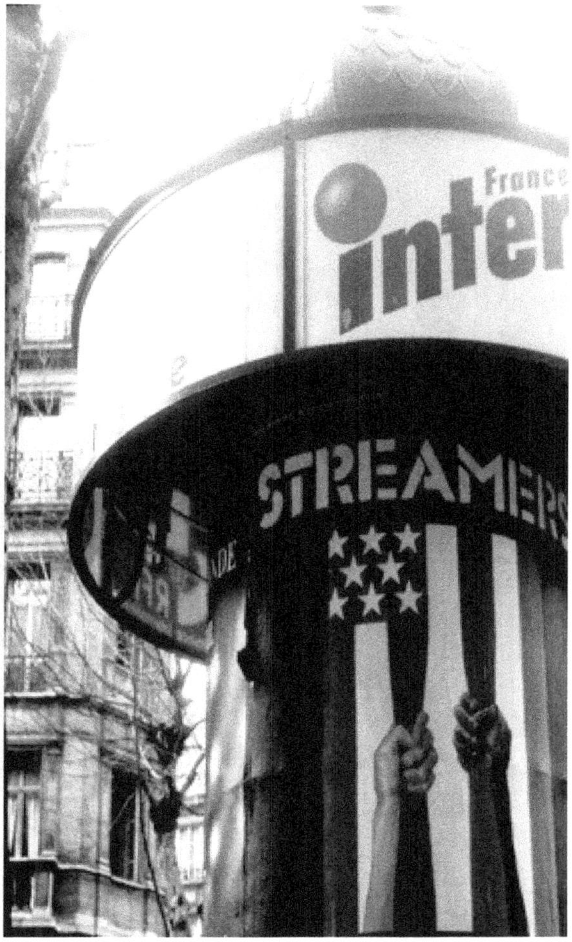
France
inter
STREAMERS

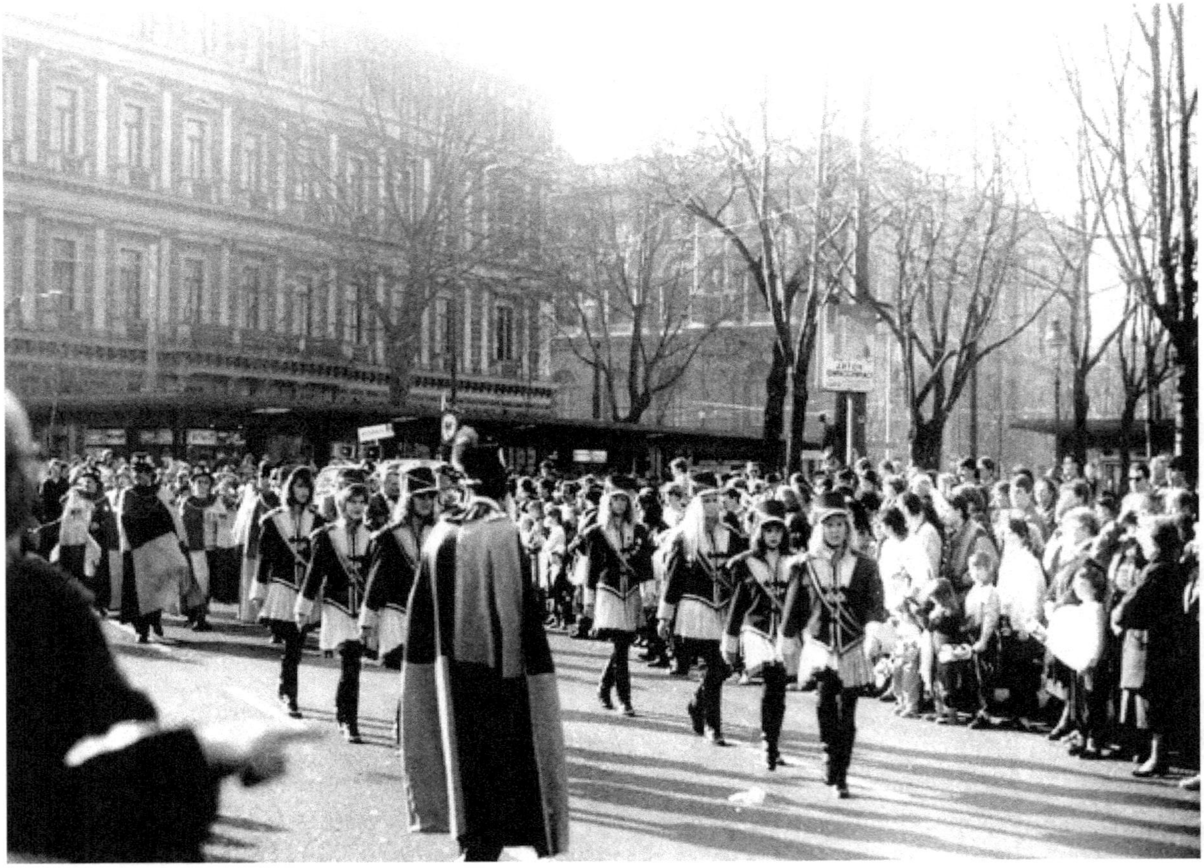

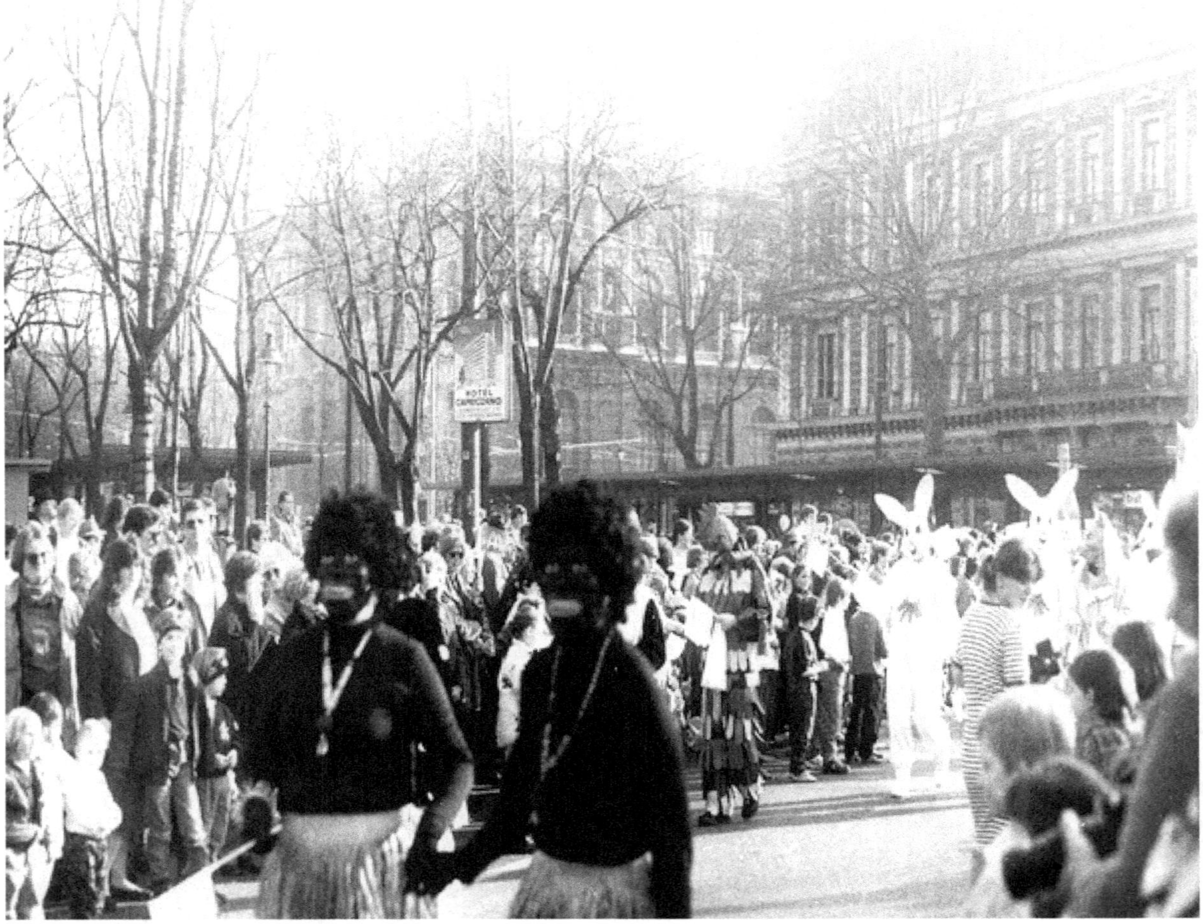
HOTEL

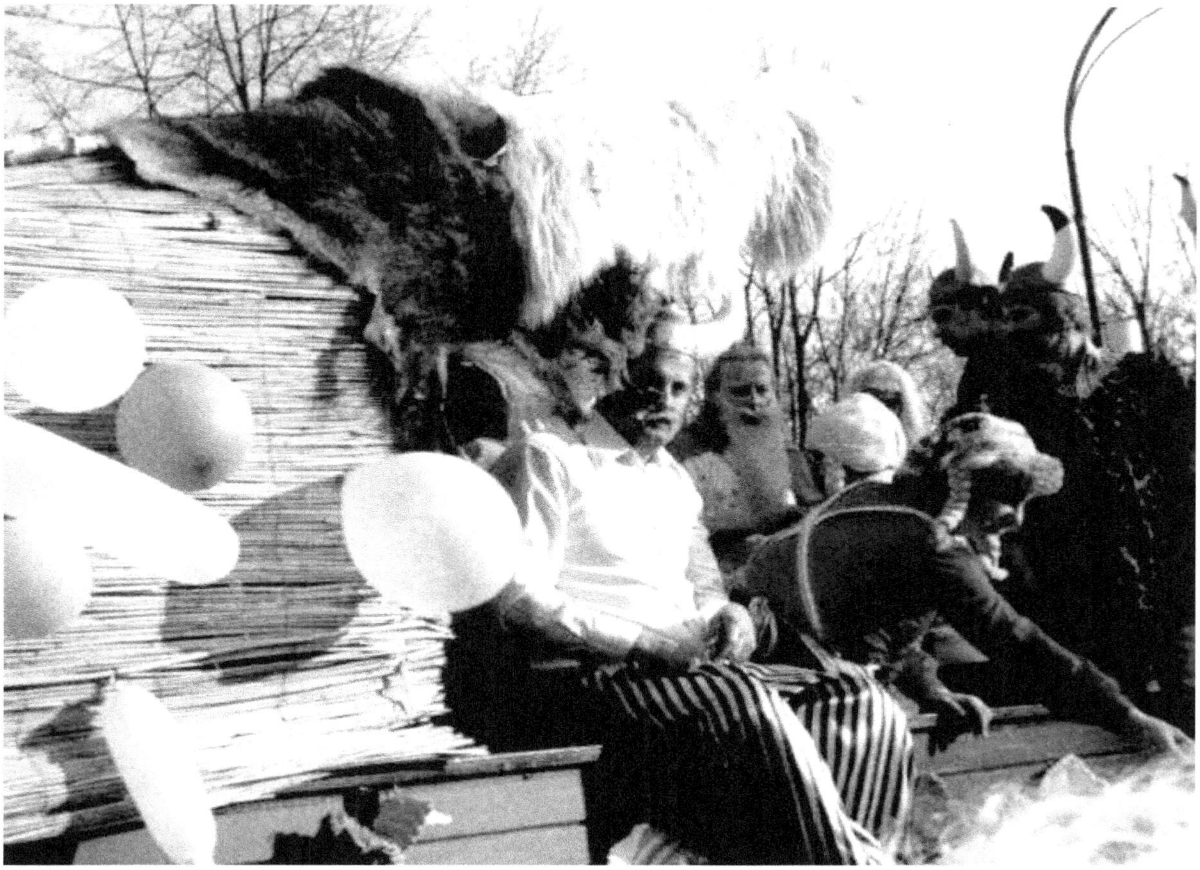

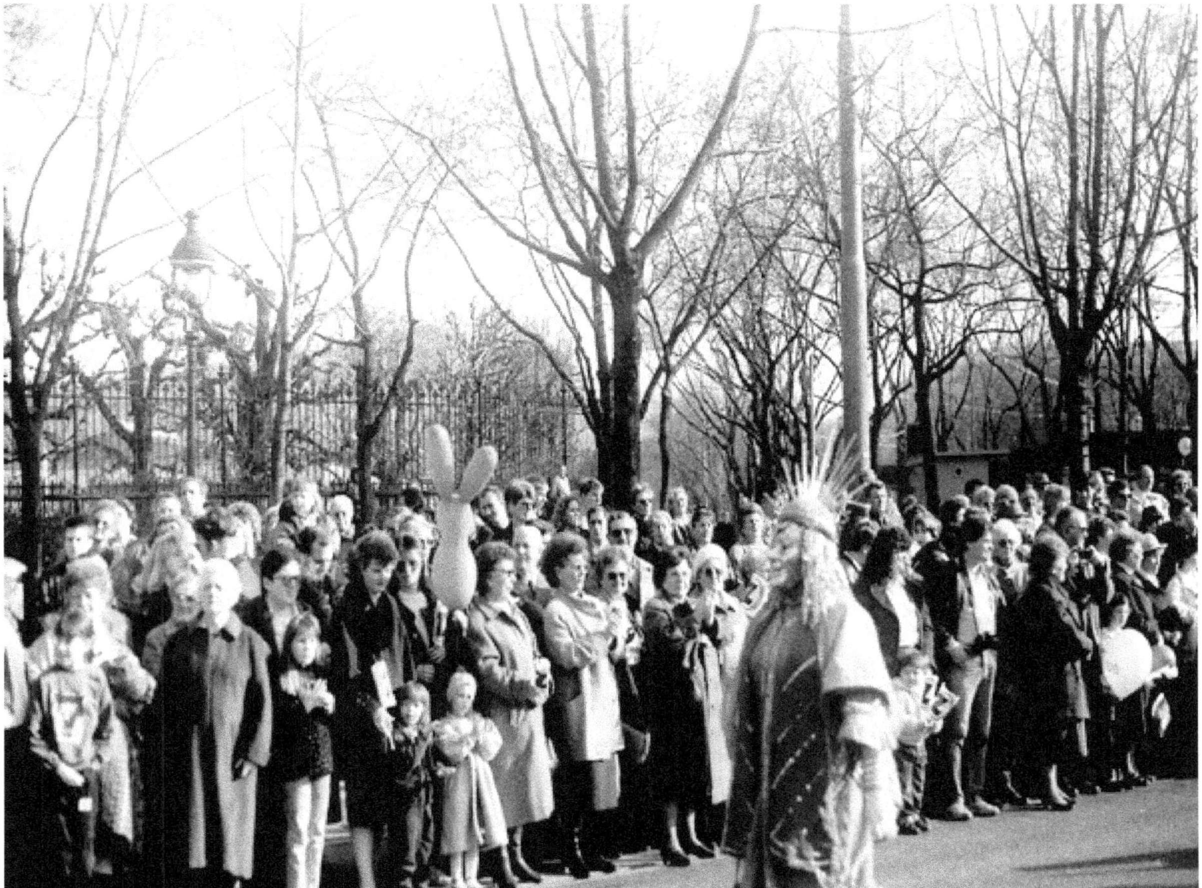

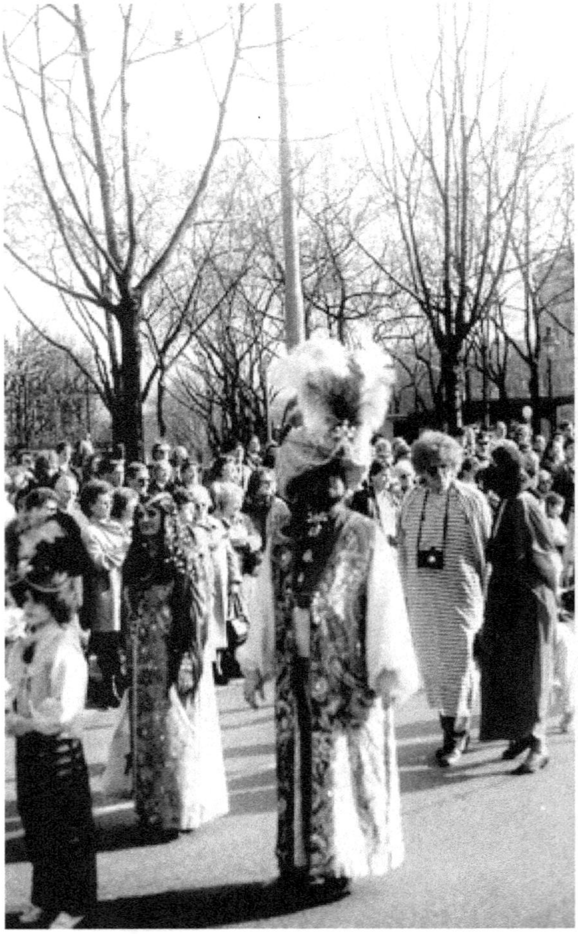

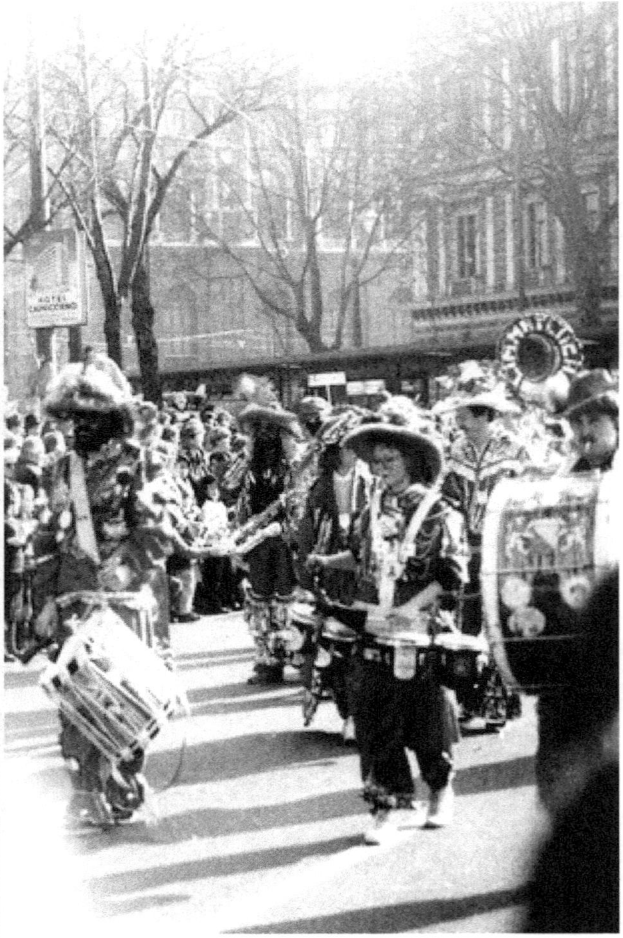

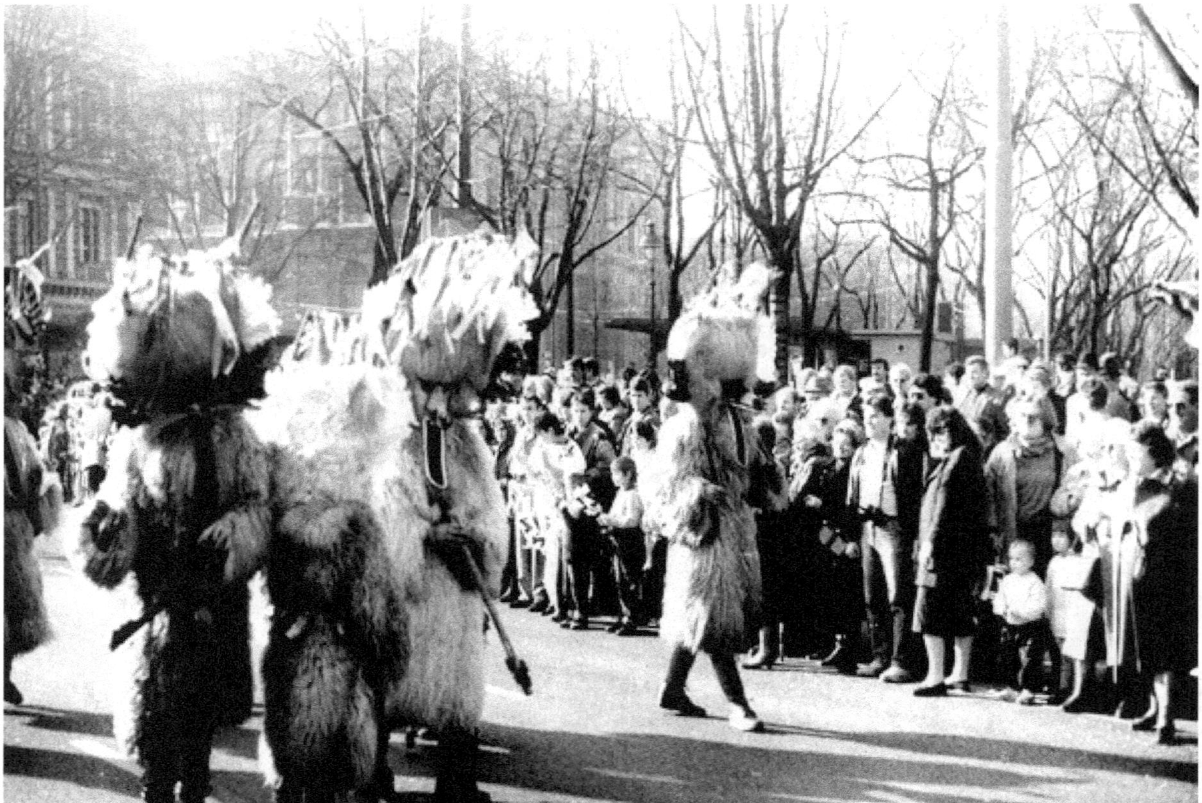

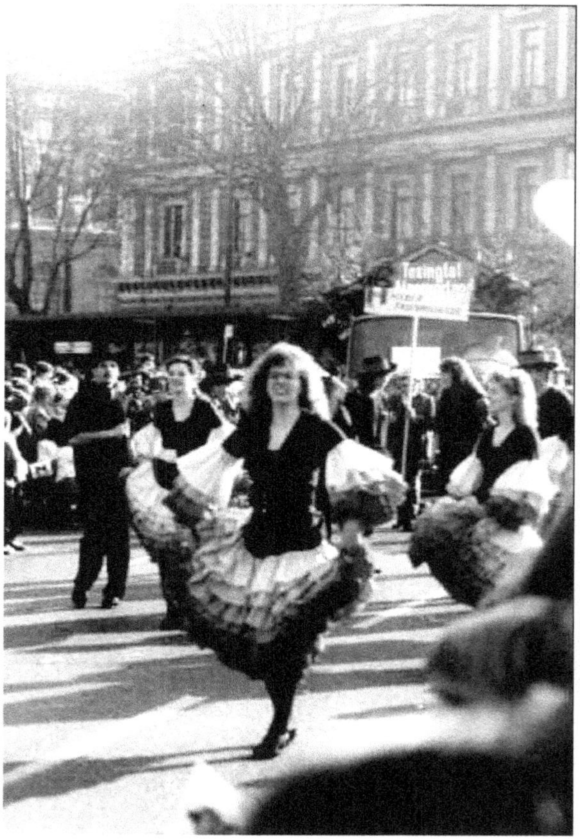
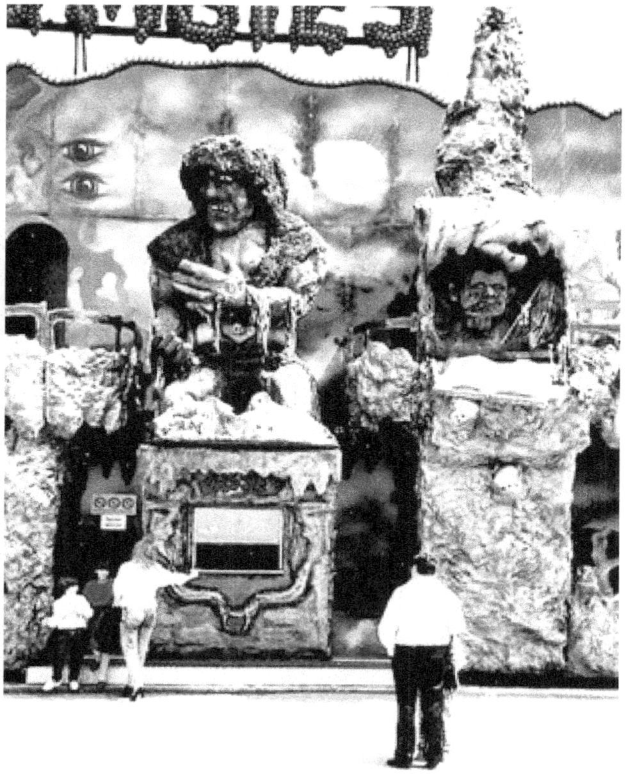
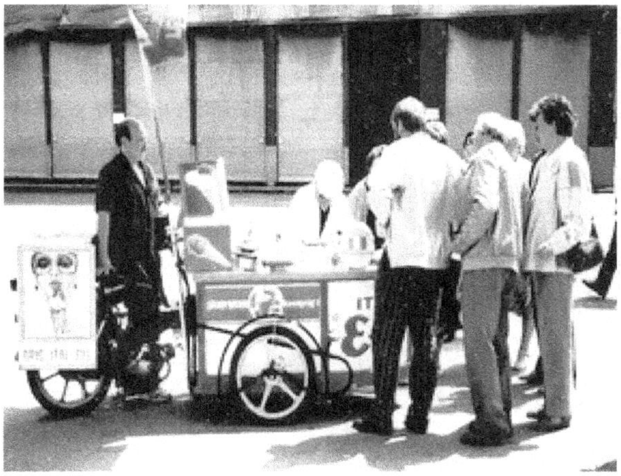
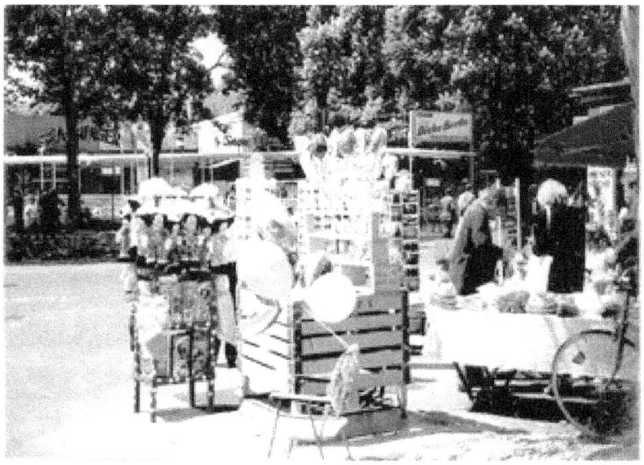
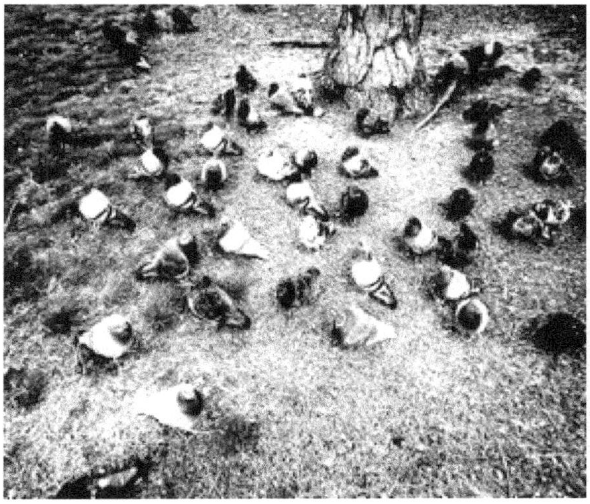
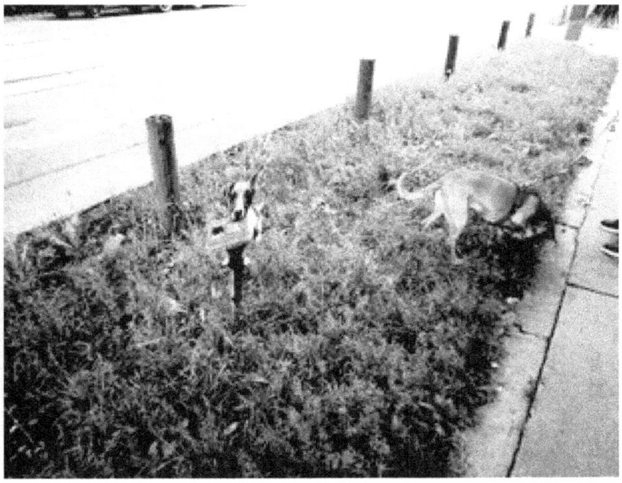

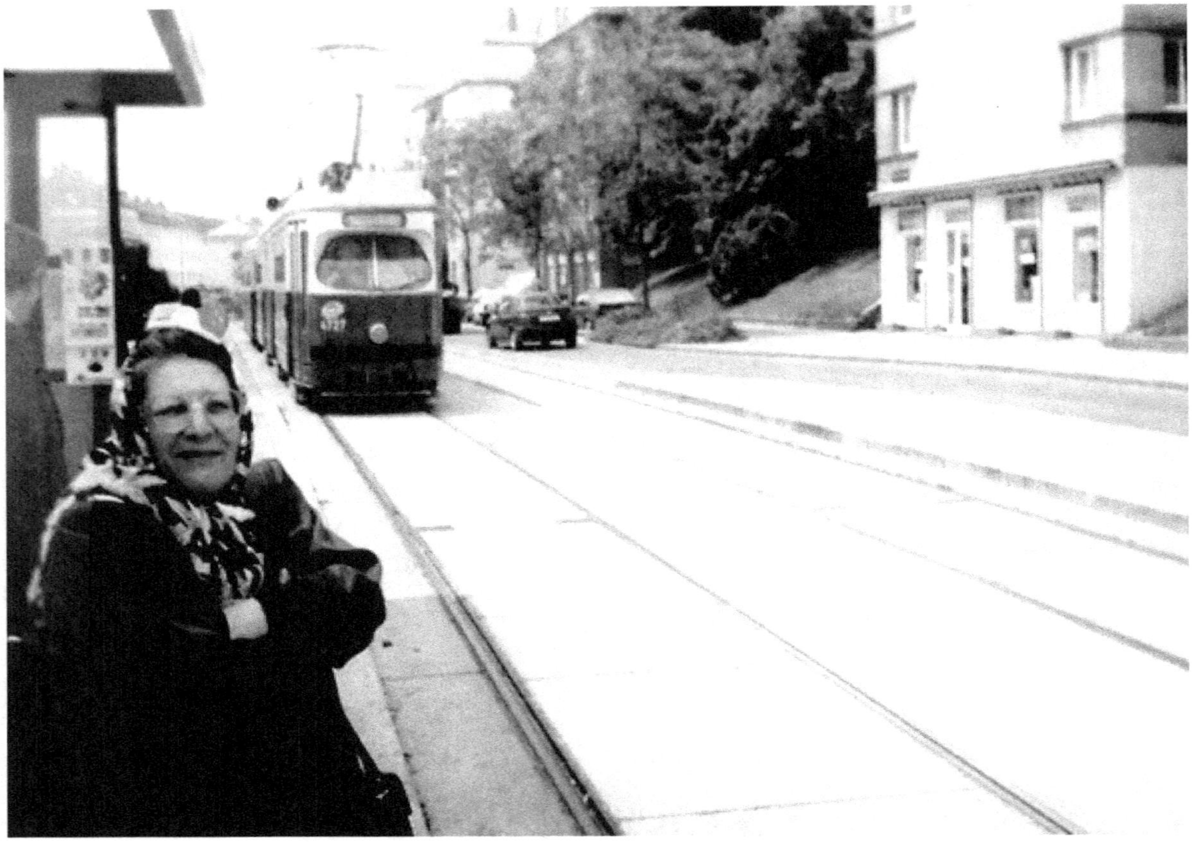

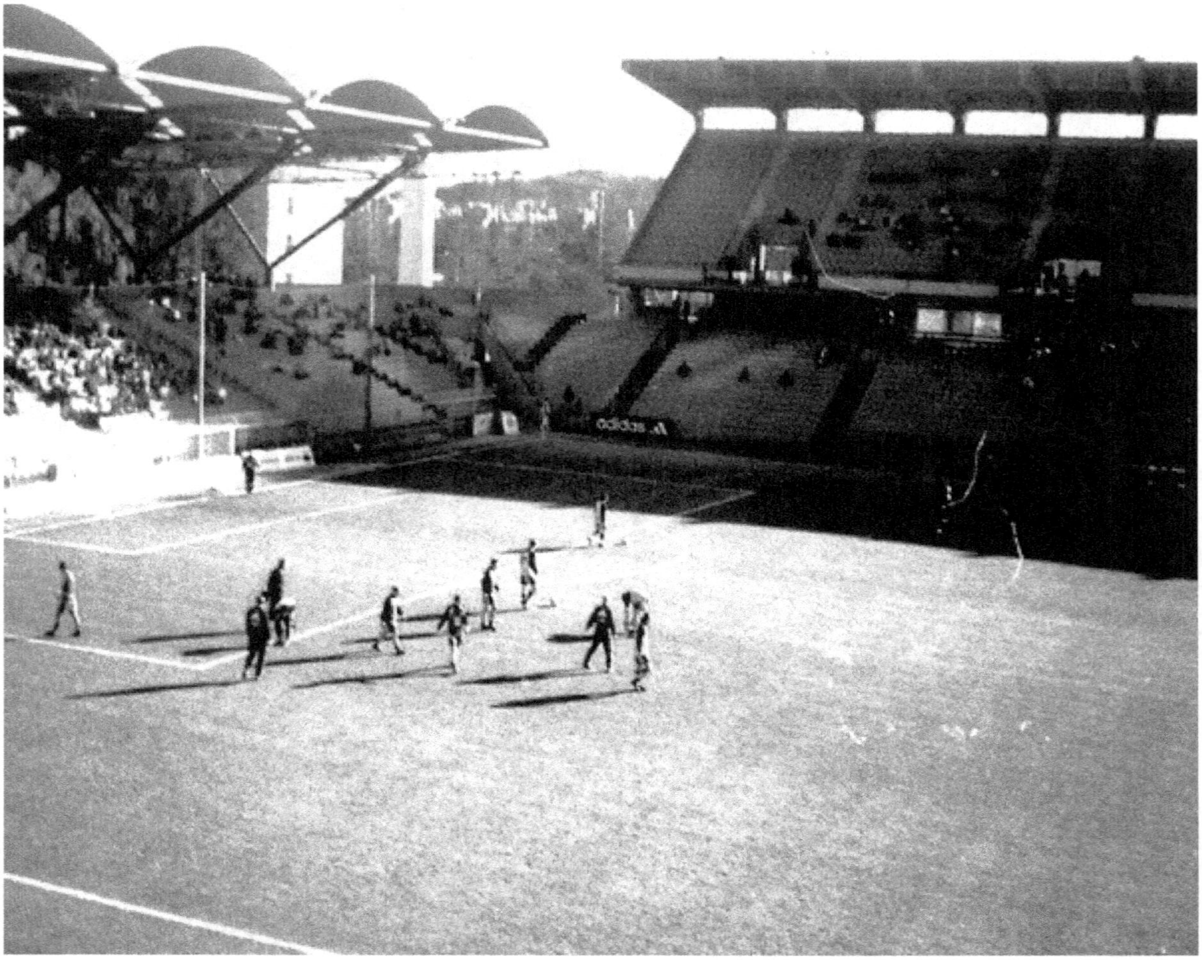
adidas

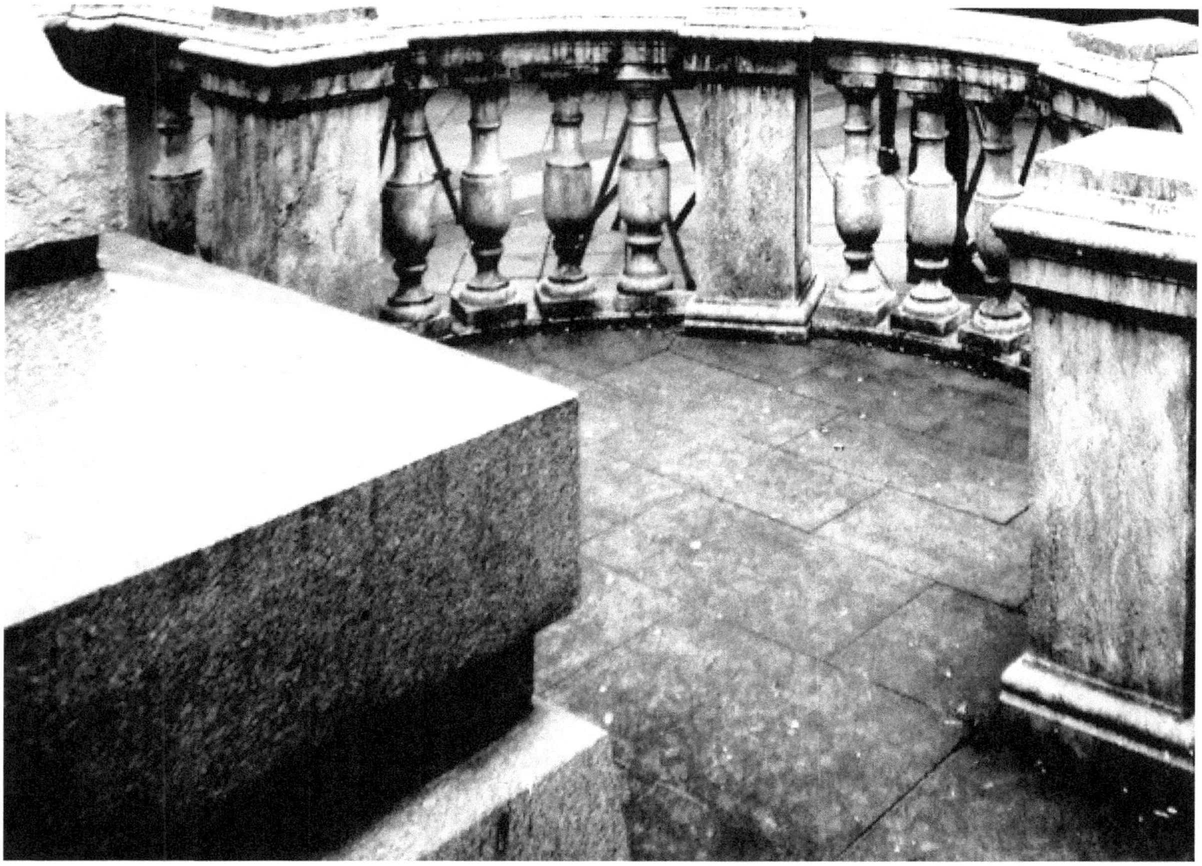

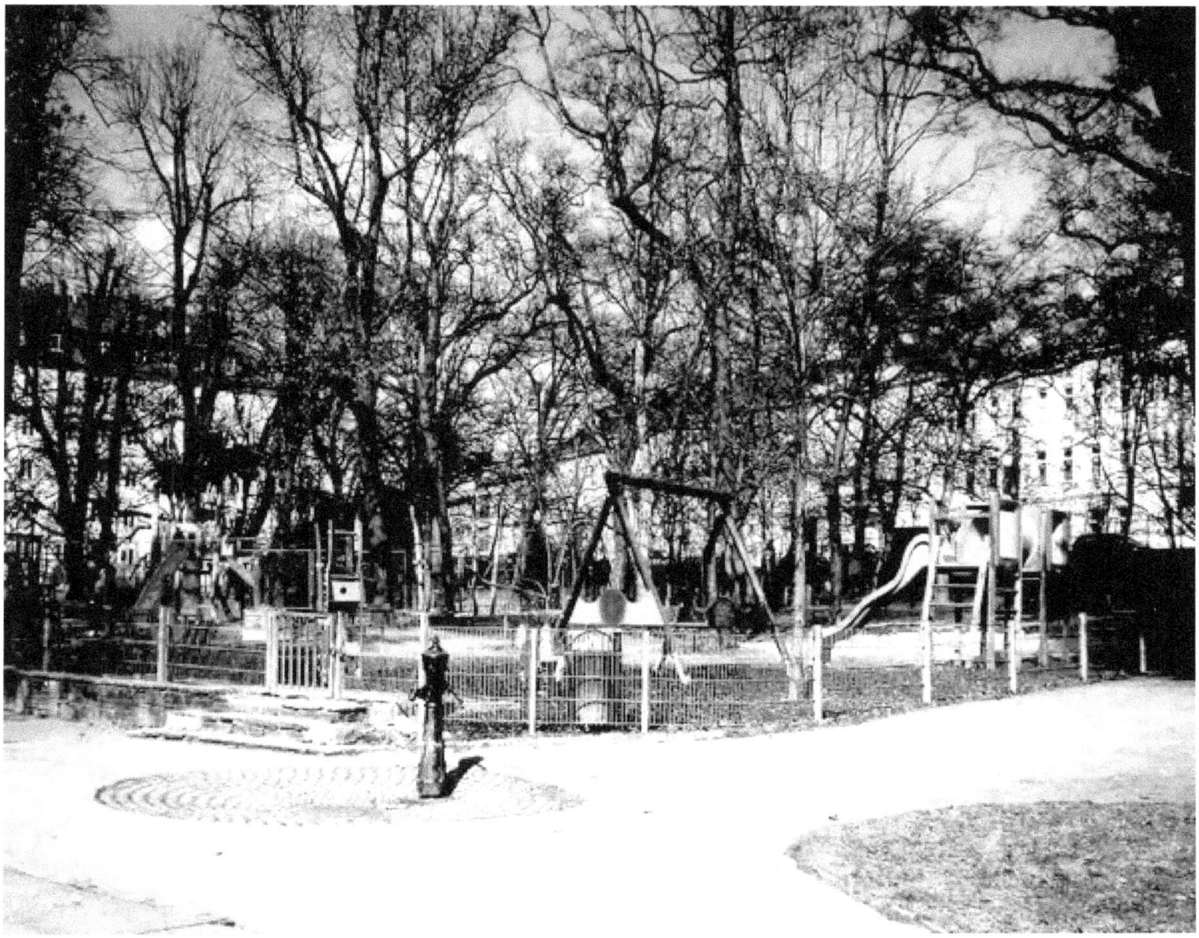

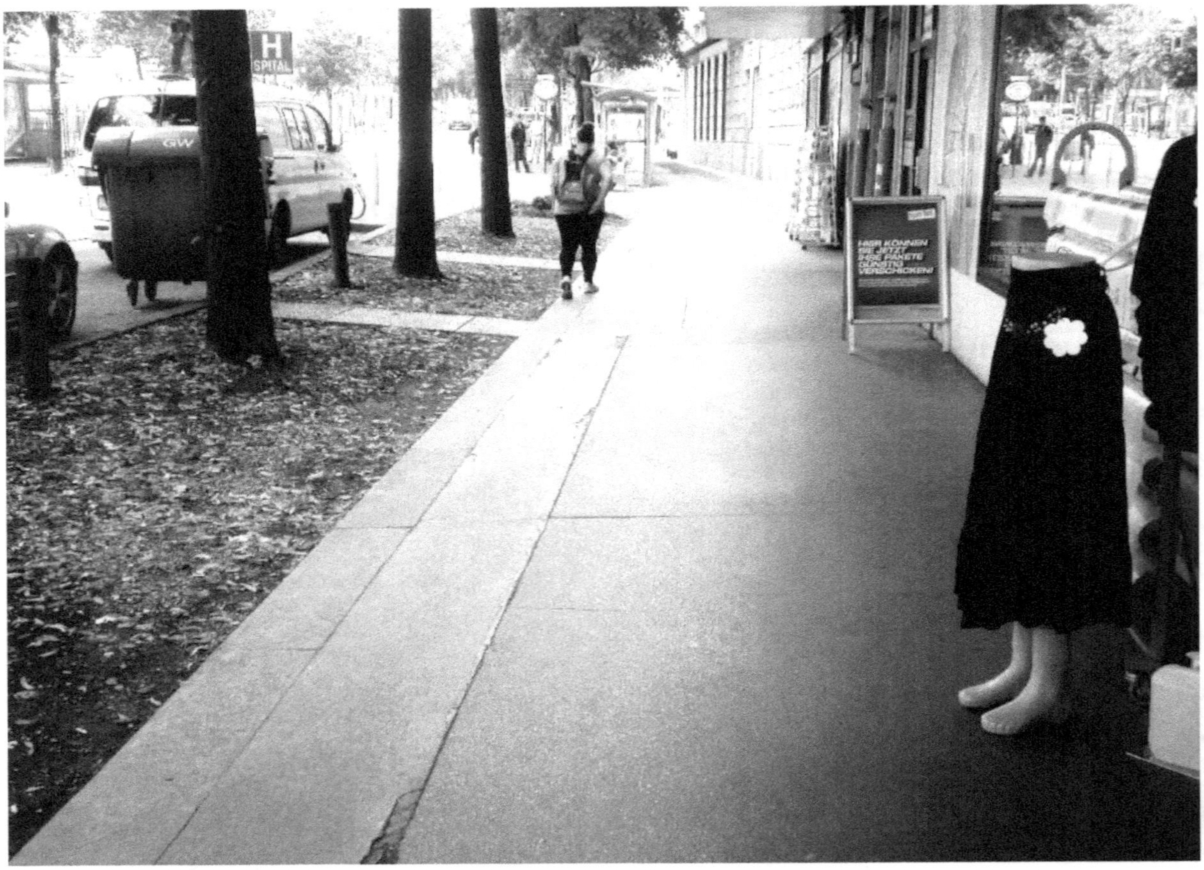
H
SPITAL
GW
HIER KÖNNEN
SIE JETZT
IHRE PAKETE
GÜNSTIG
VERSCHICKEN!

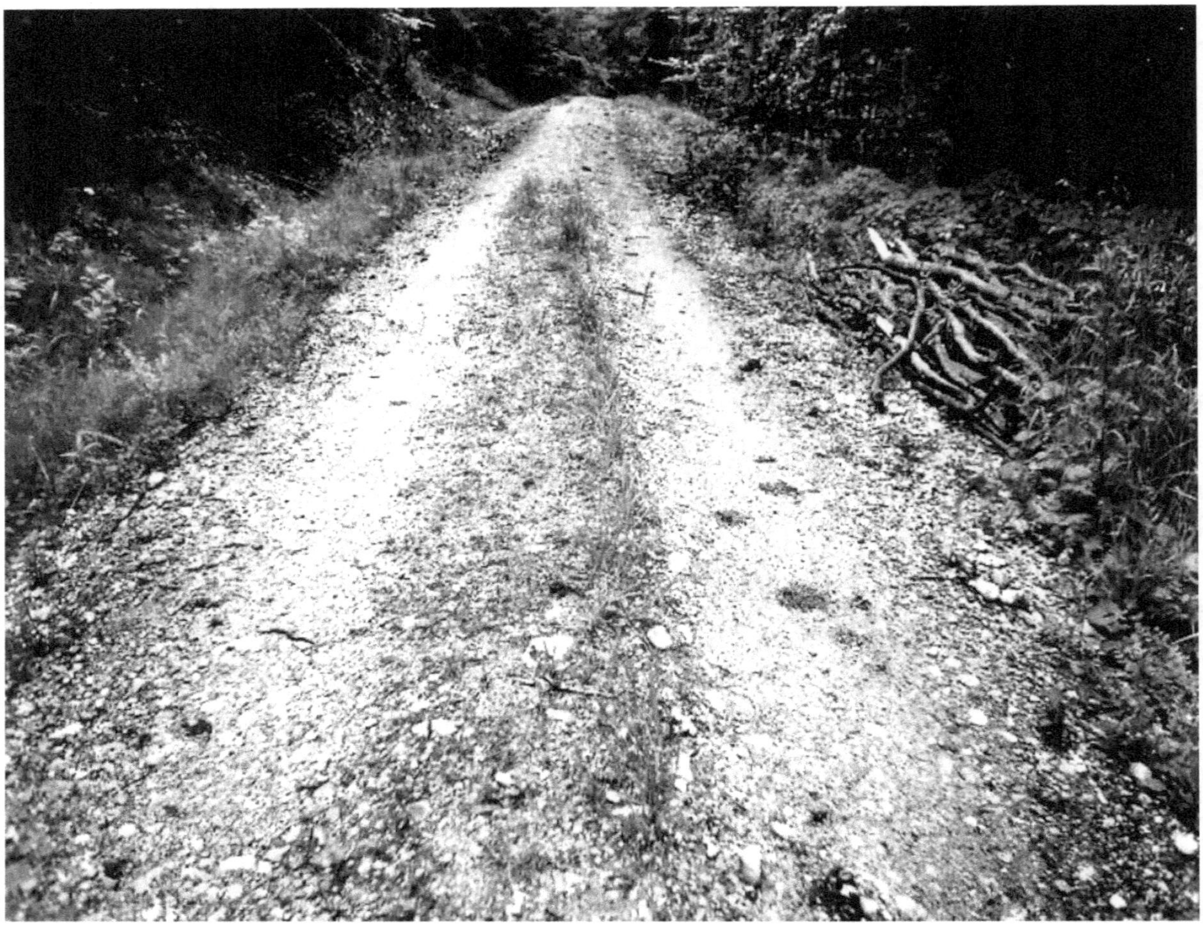

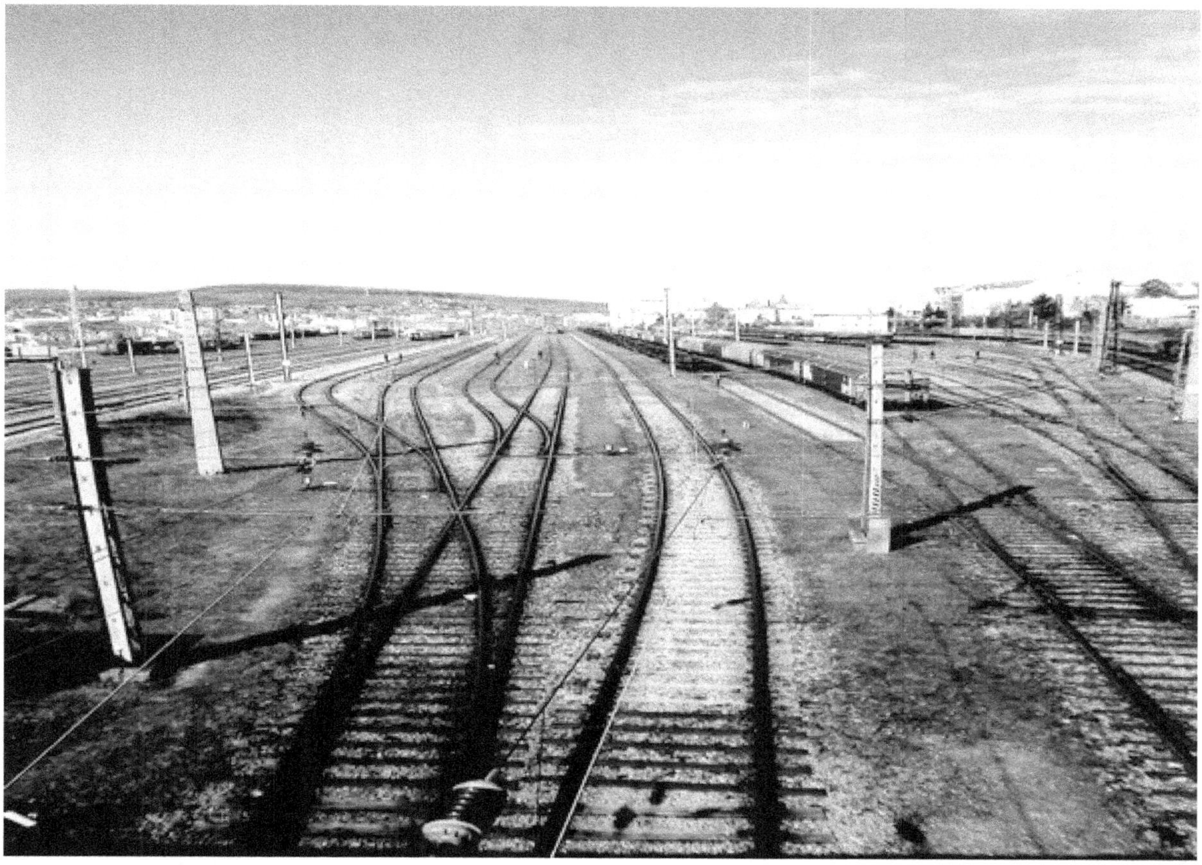

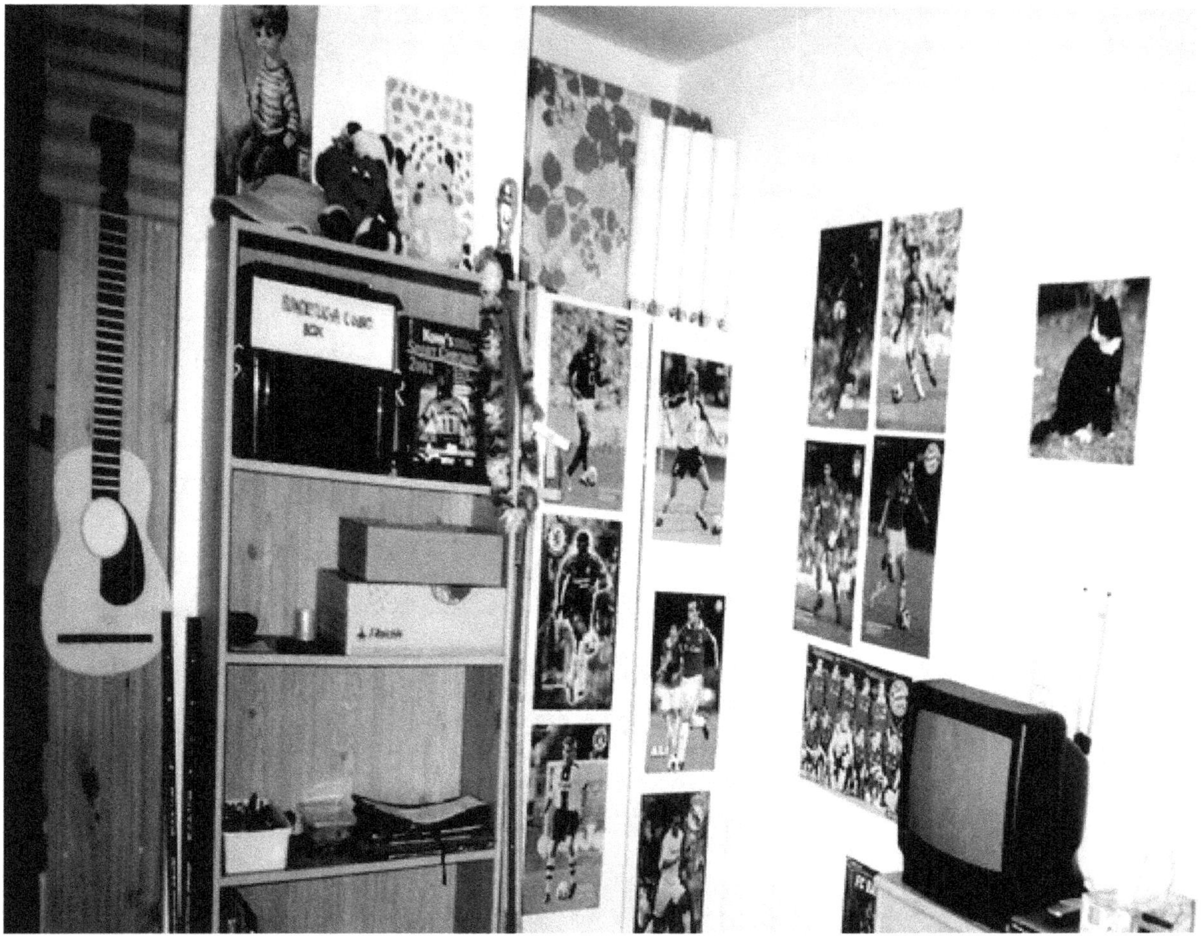

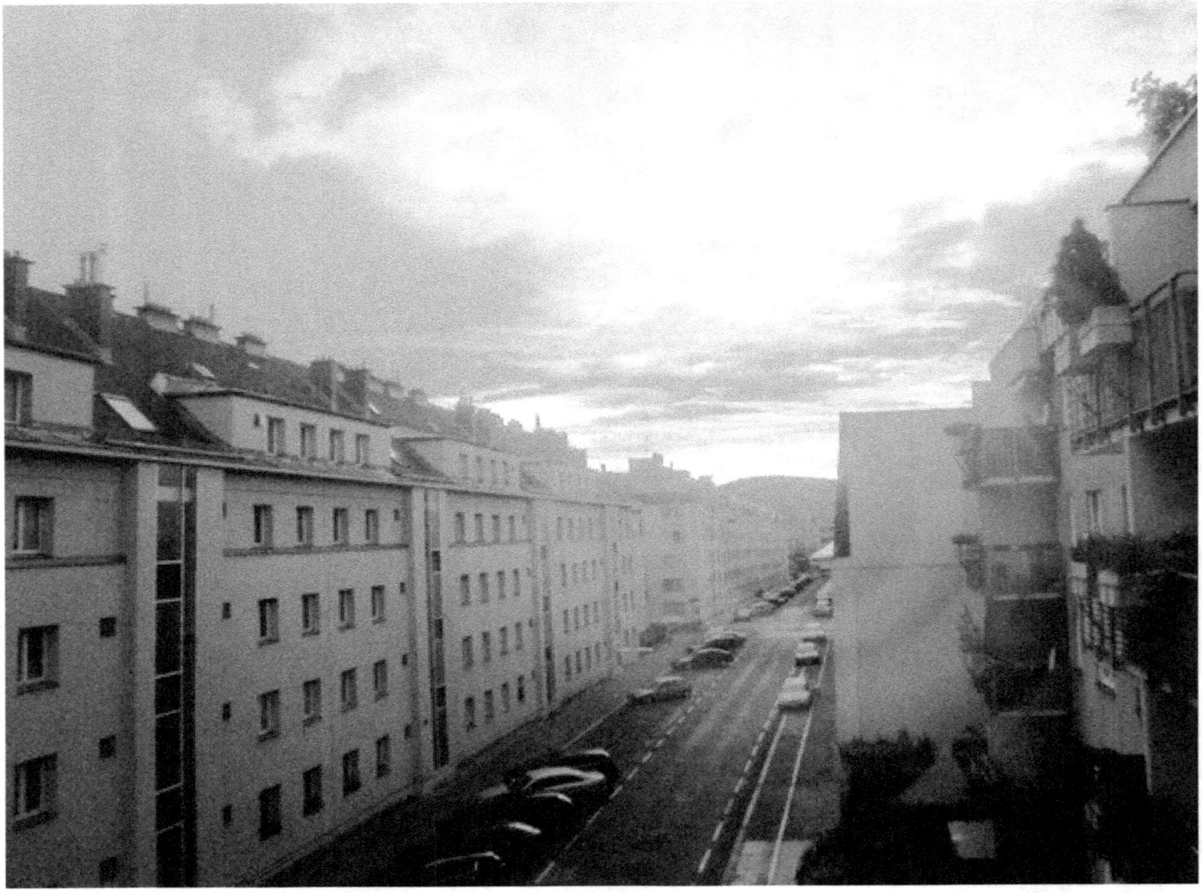

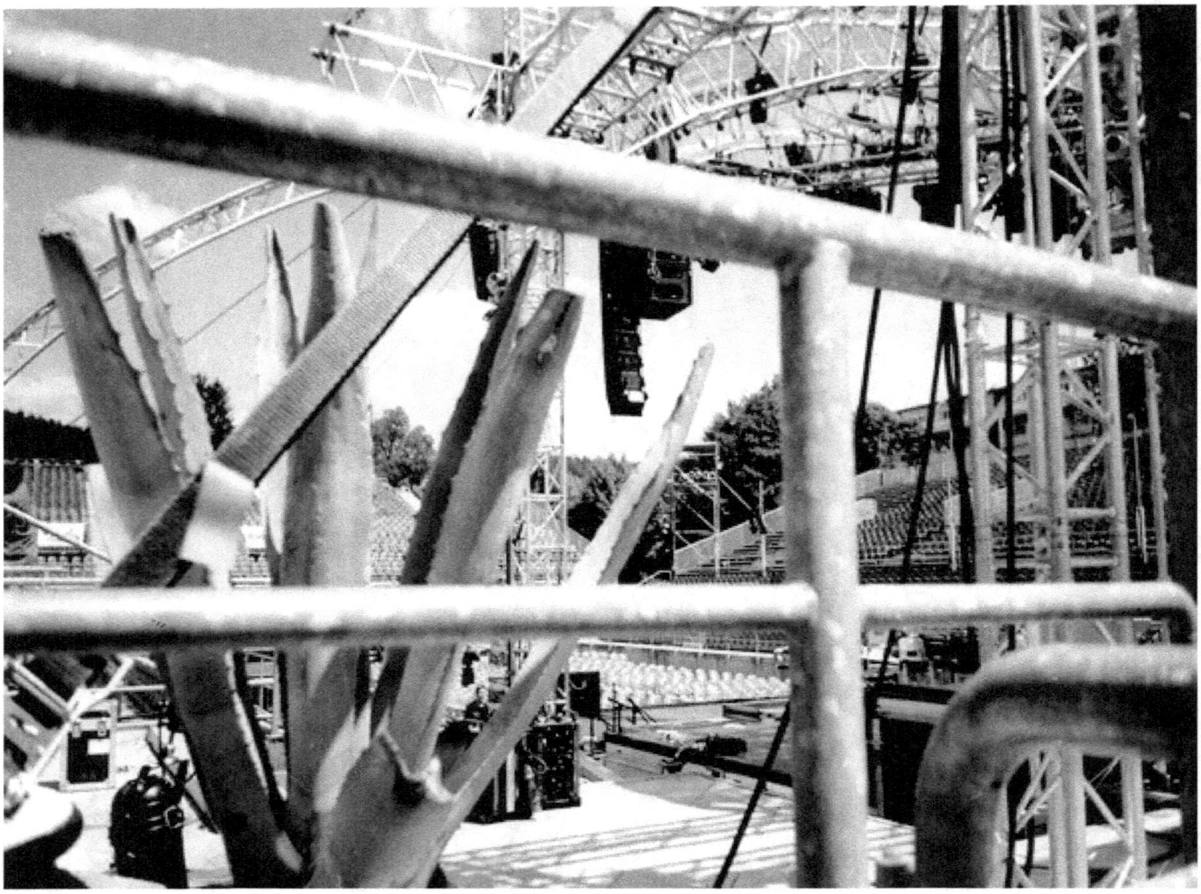

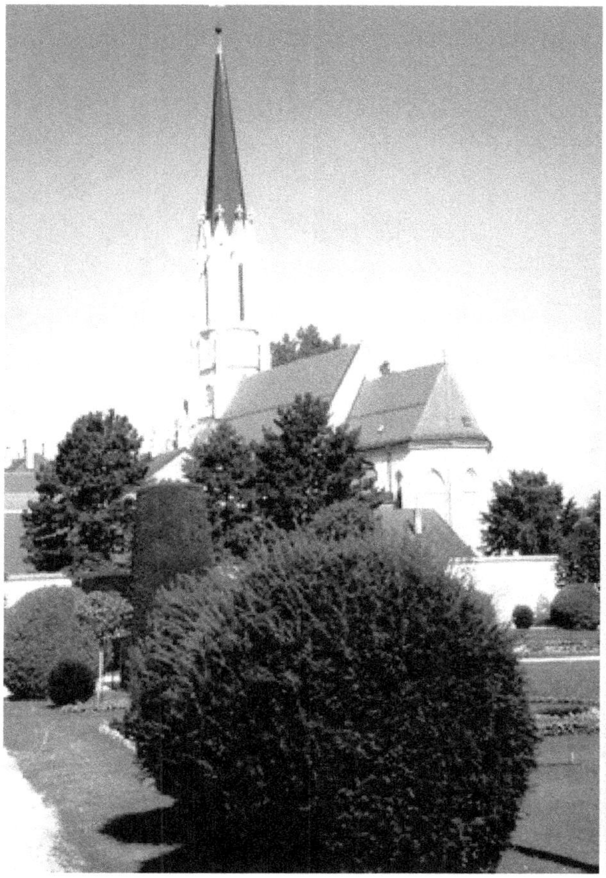

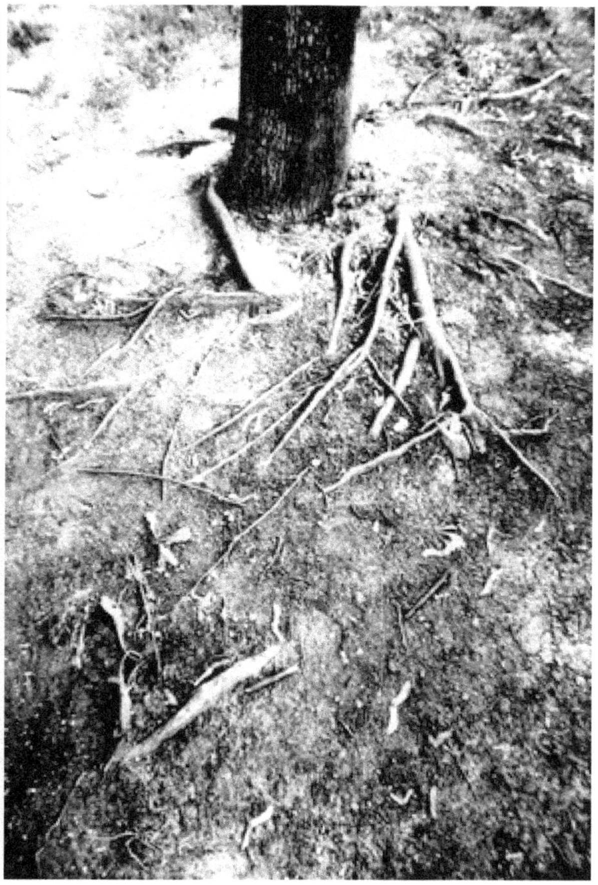

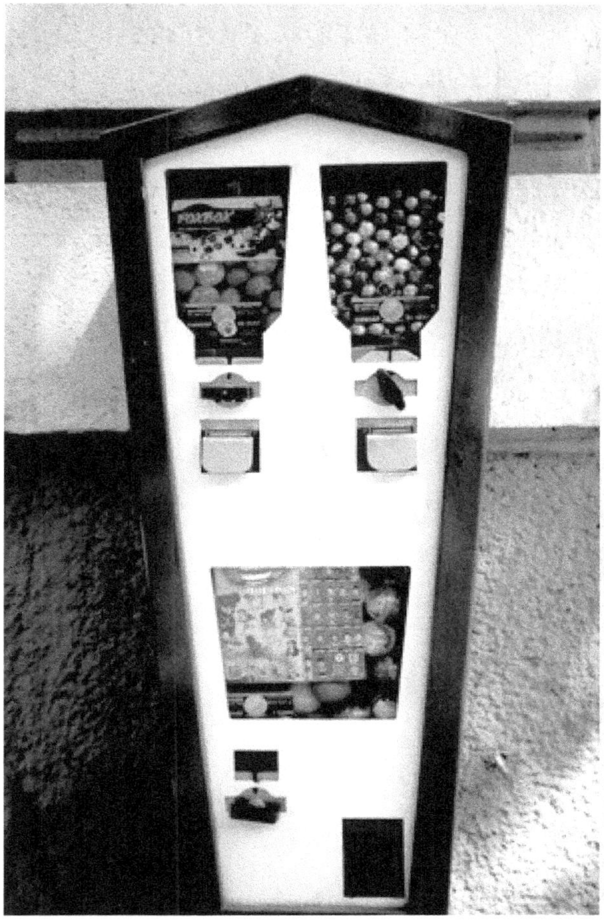

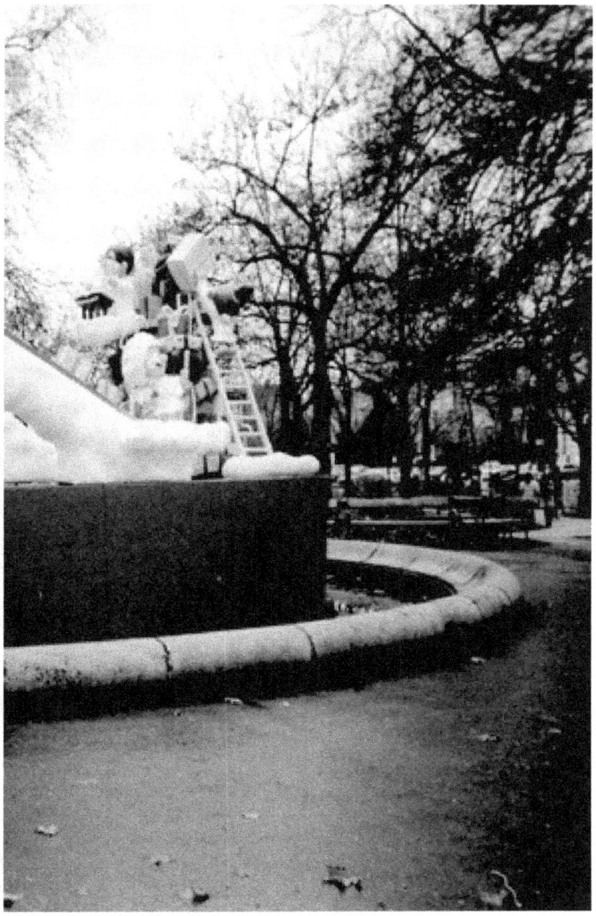

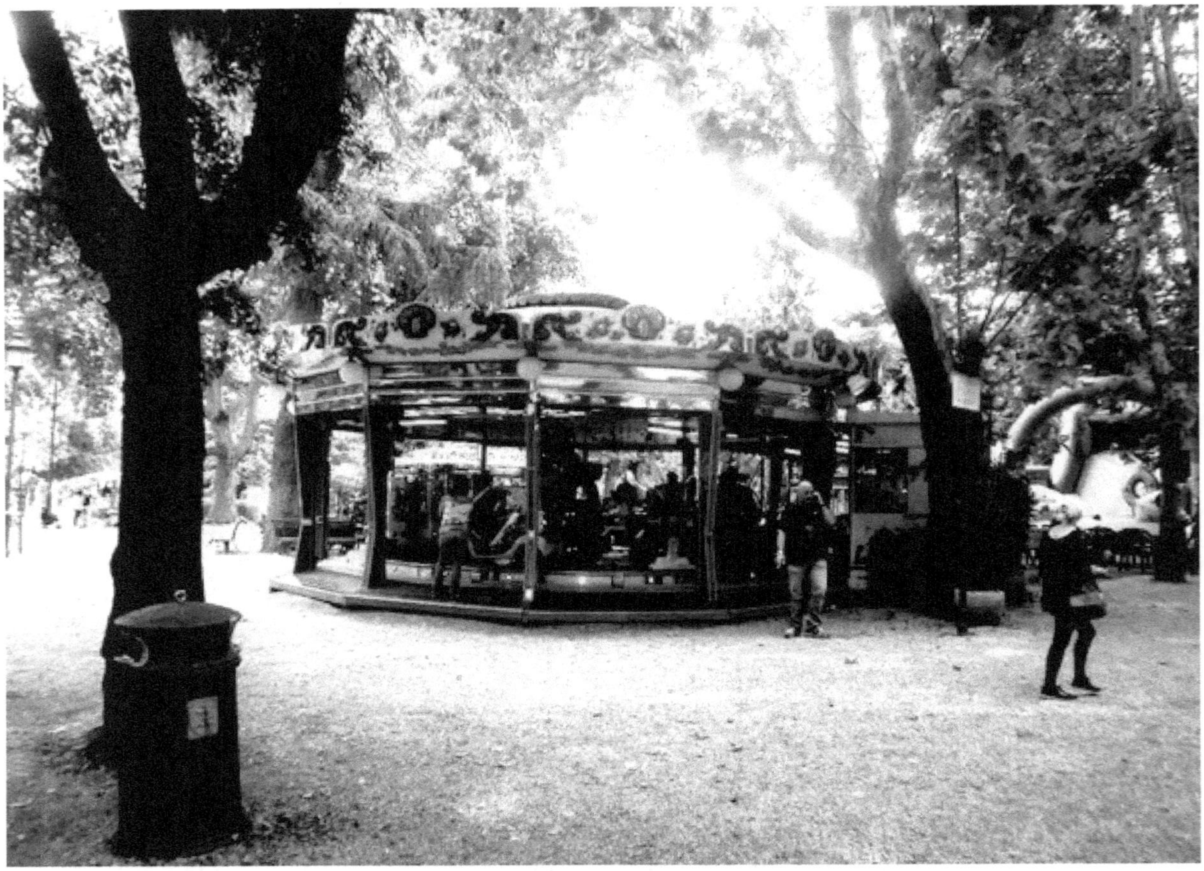

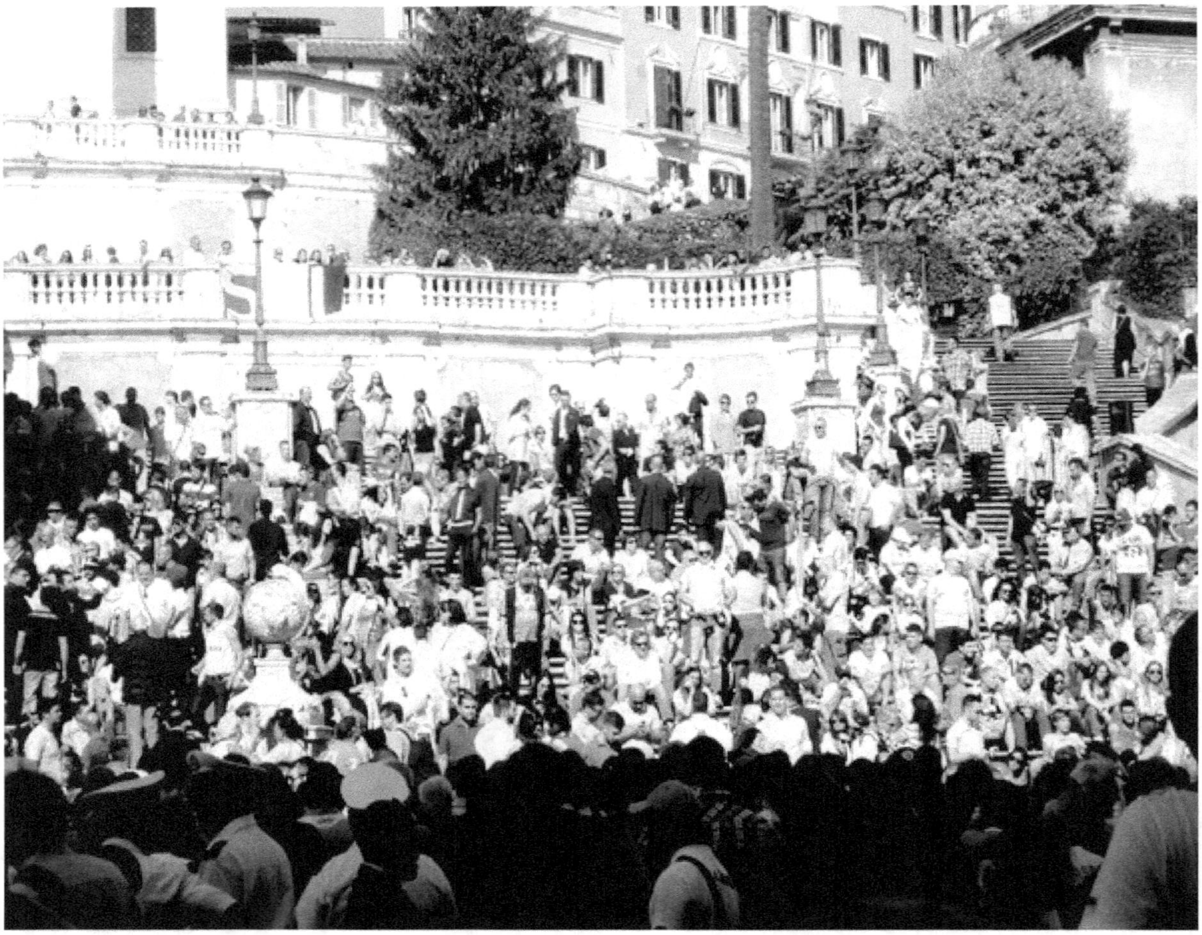

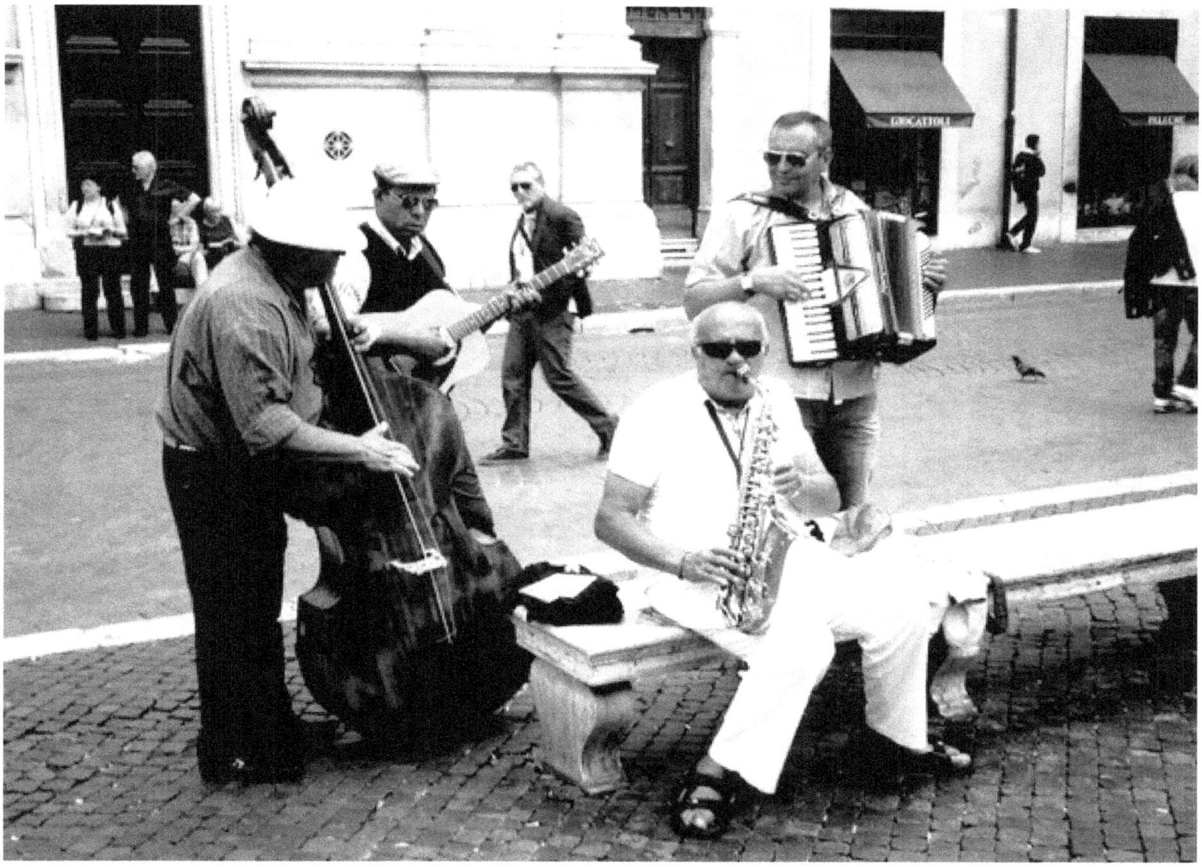

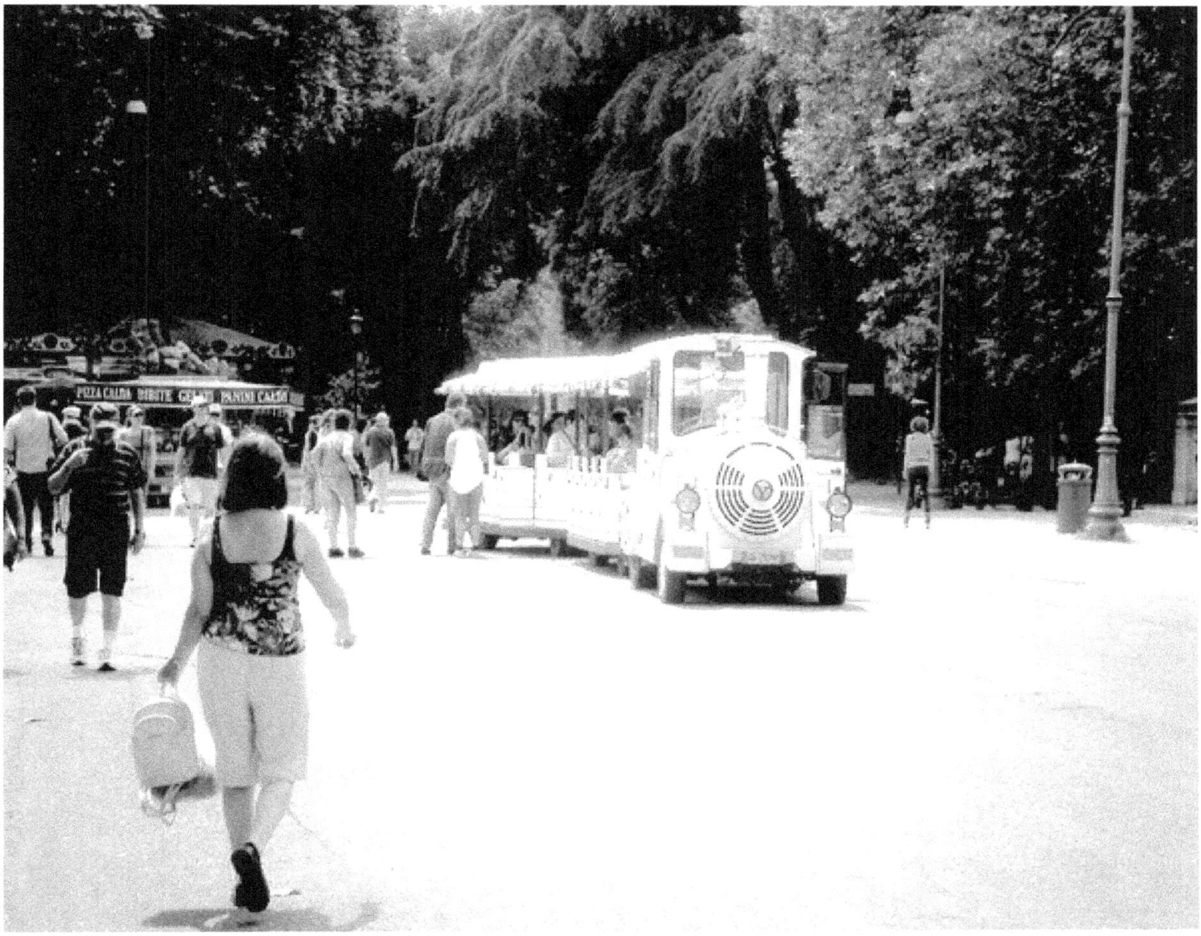

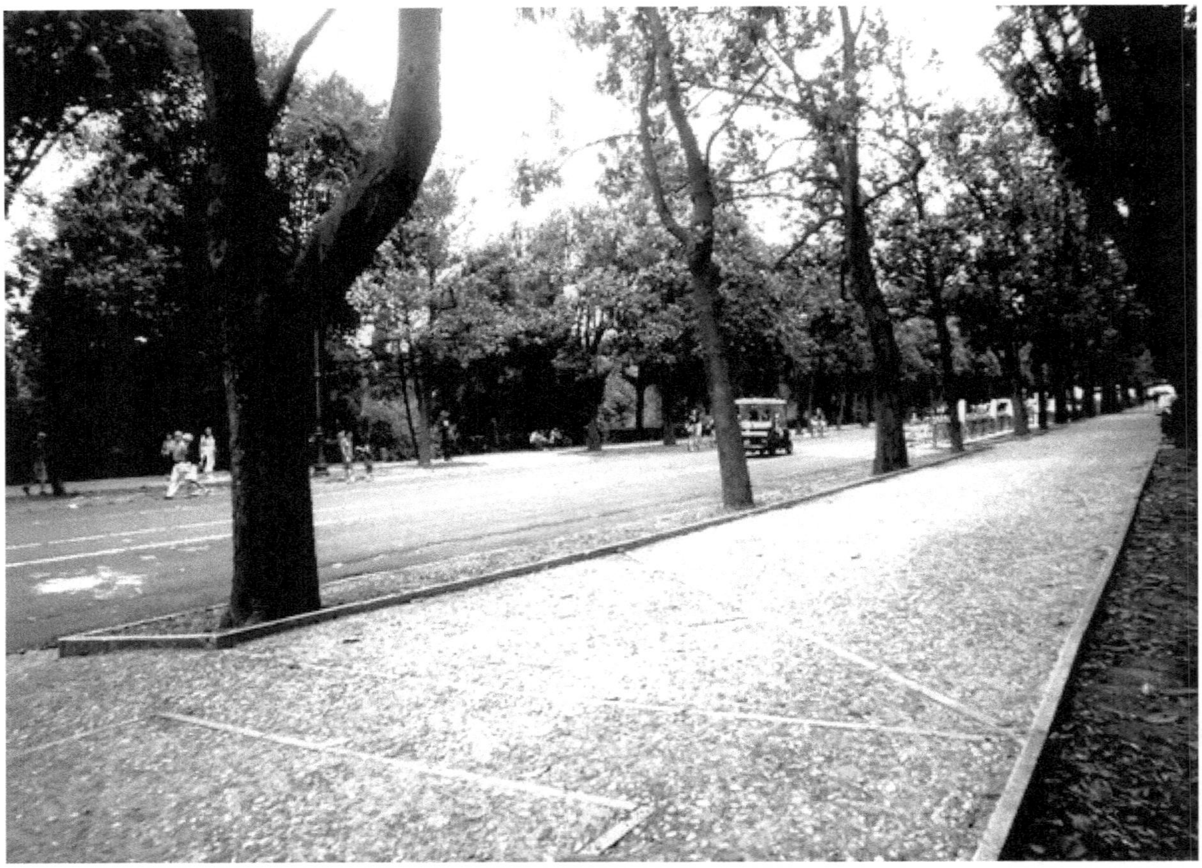

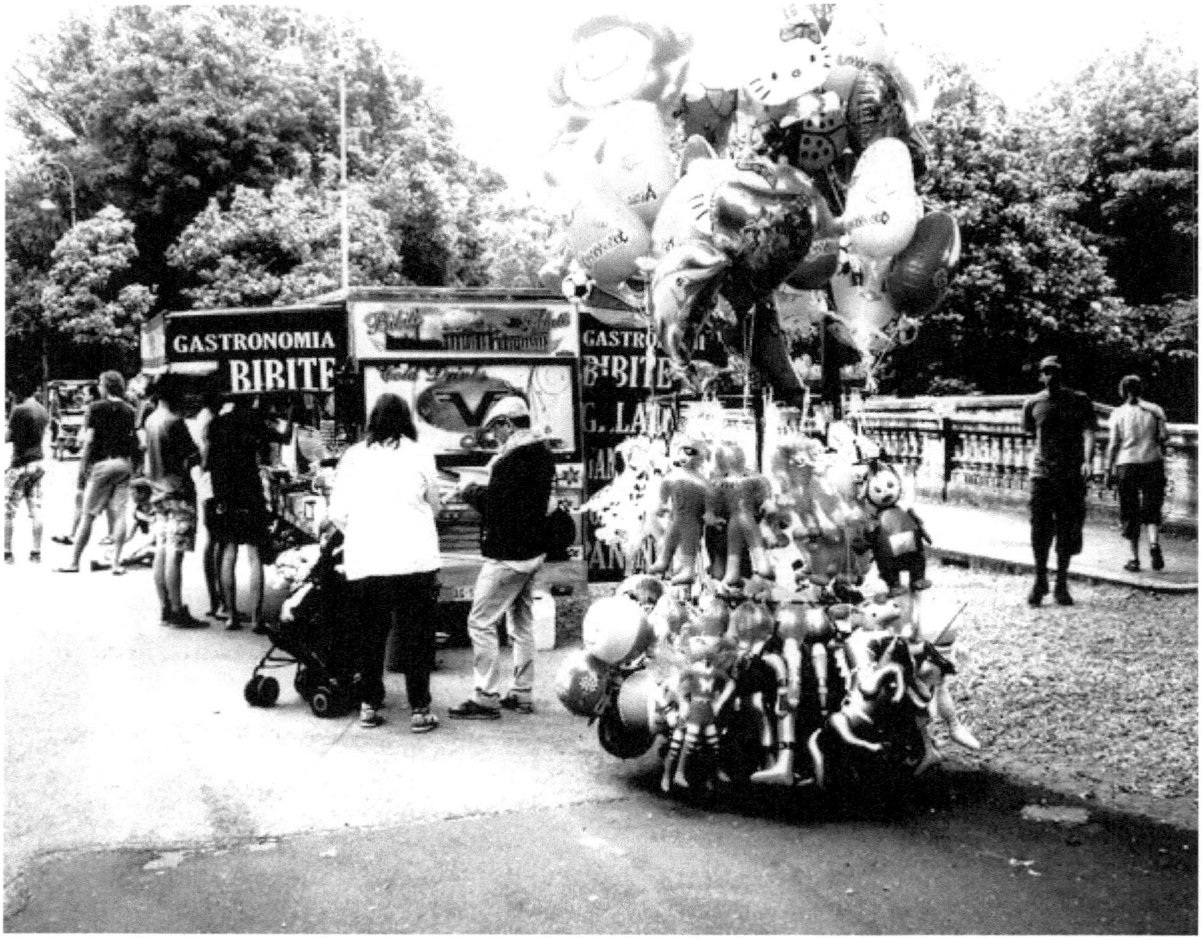
GASTRONOMIA
BIBITE
BIBITE

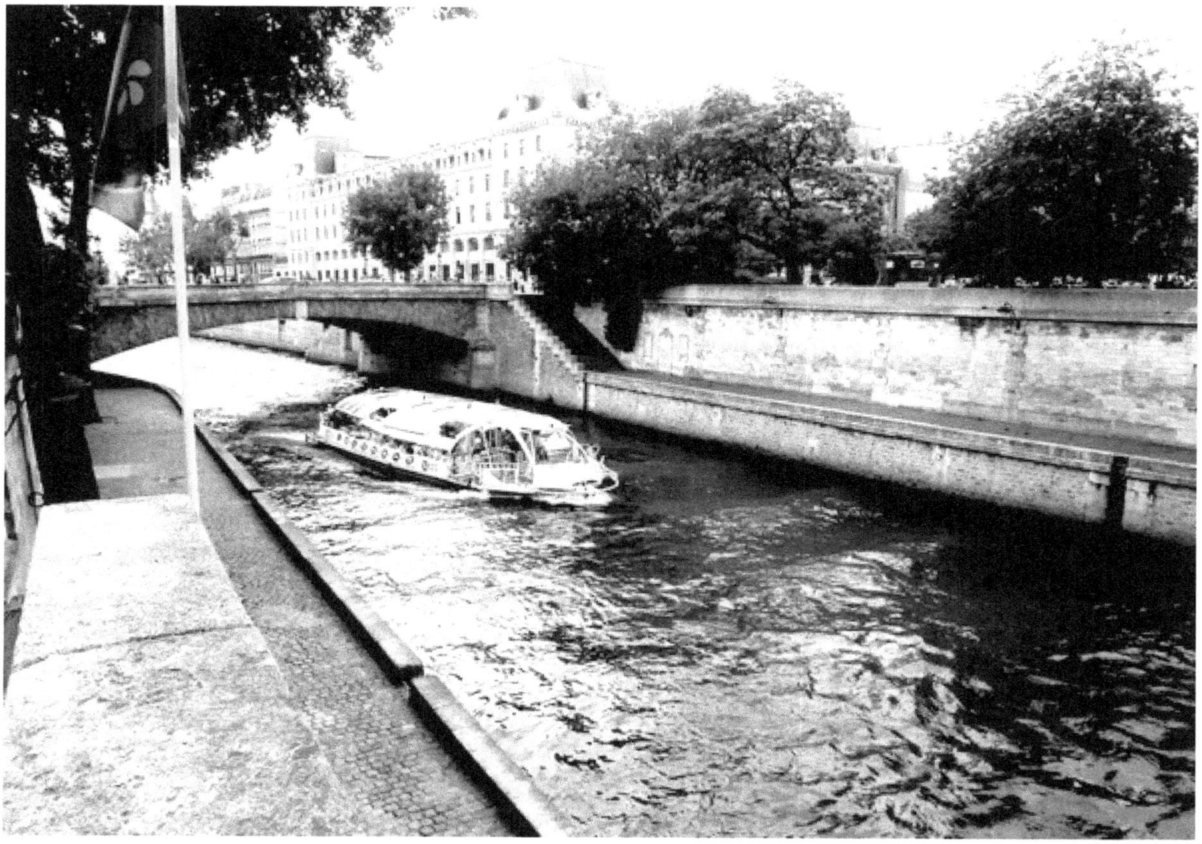

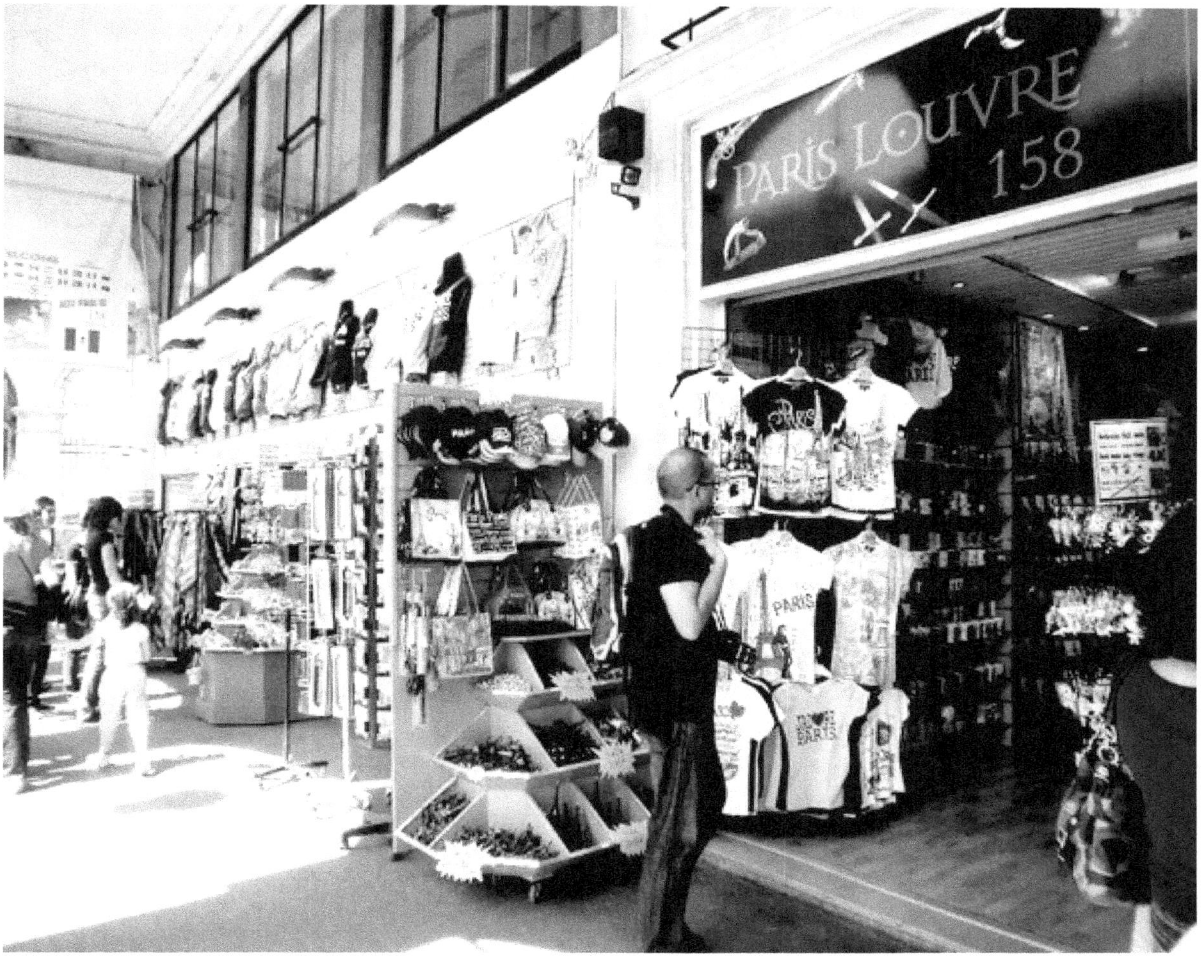
PARIS LOUVRE
158
PARIS

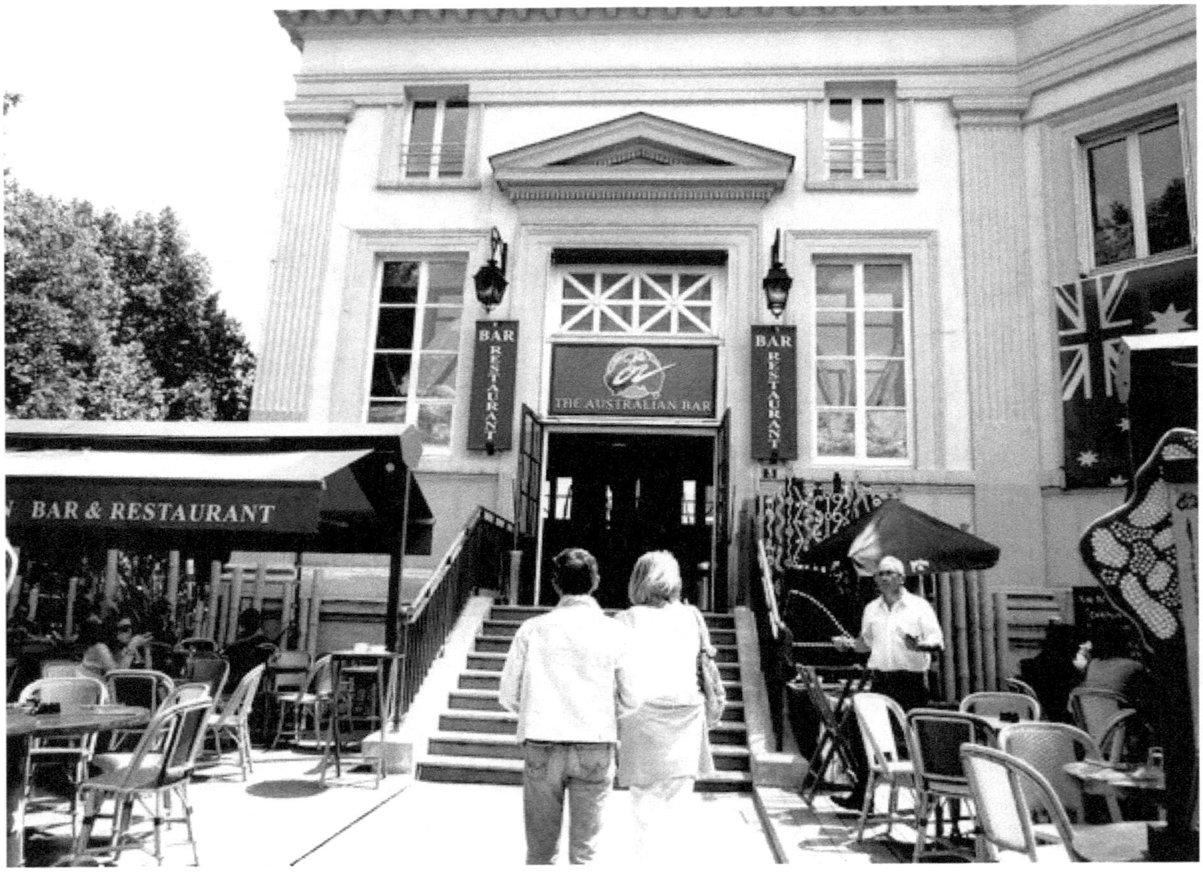
BAR
RESTAURANT
THE AUSTRALIAN BAR
BAR
RESTAURANT
BAR & RESTAURANT

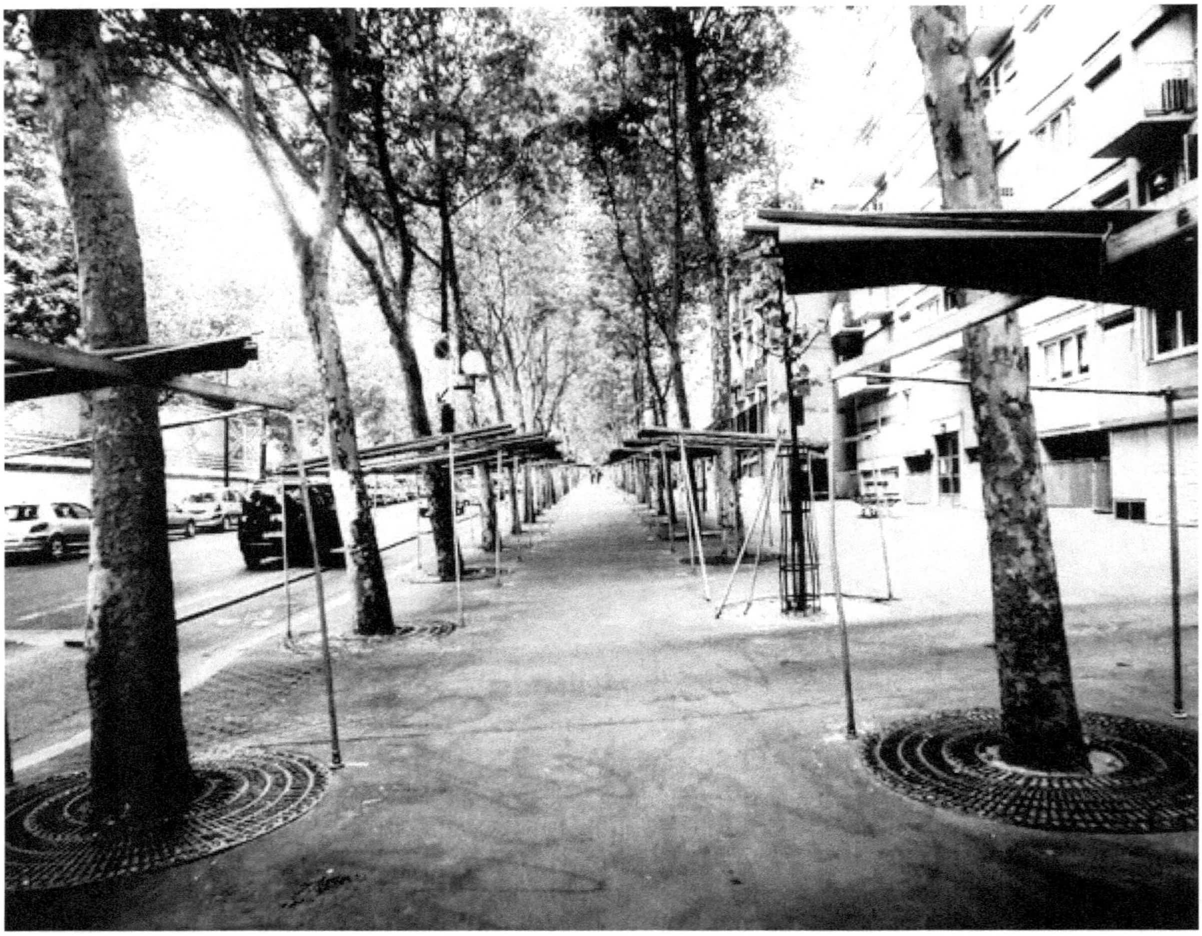

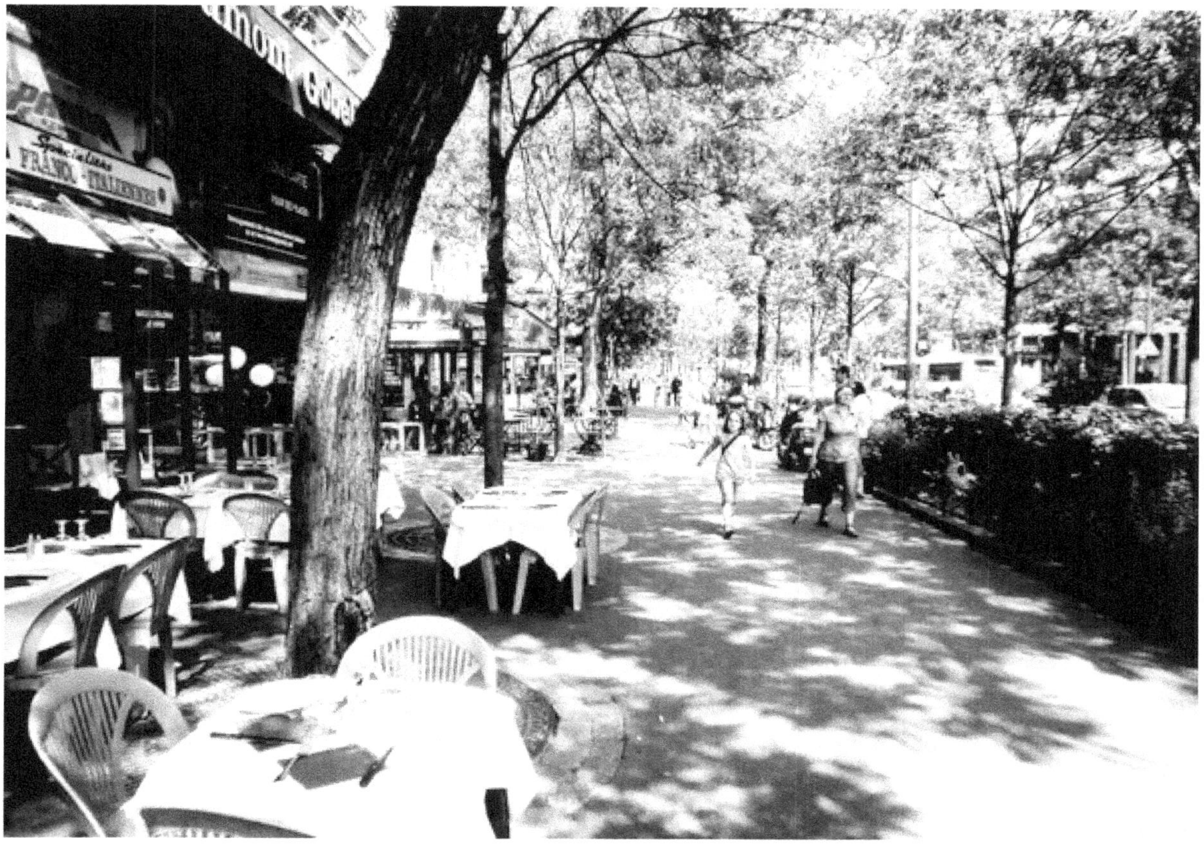

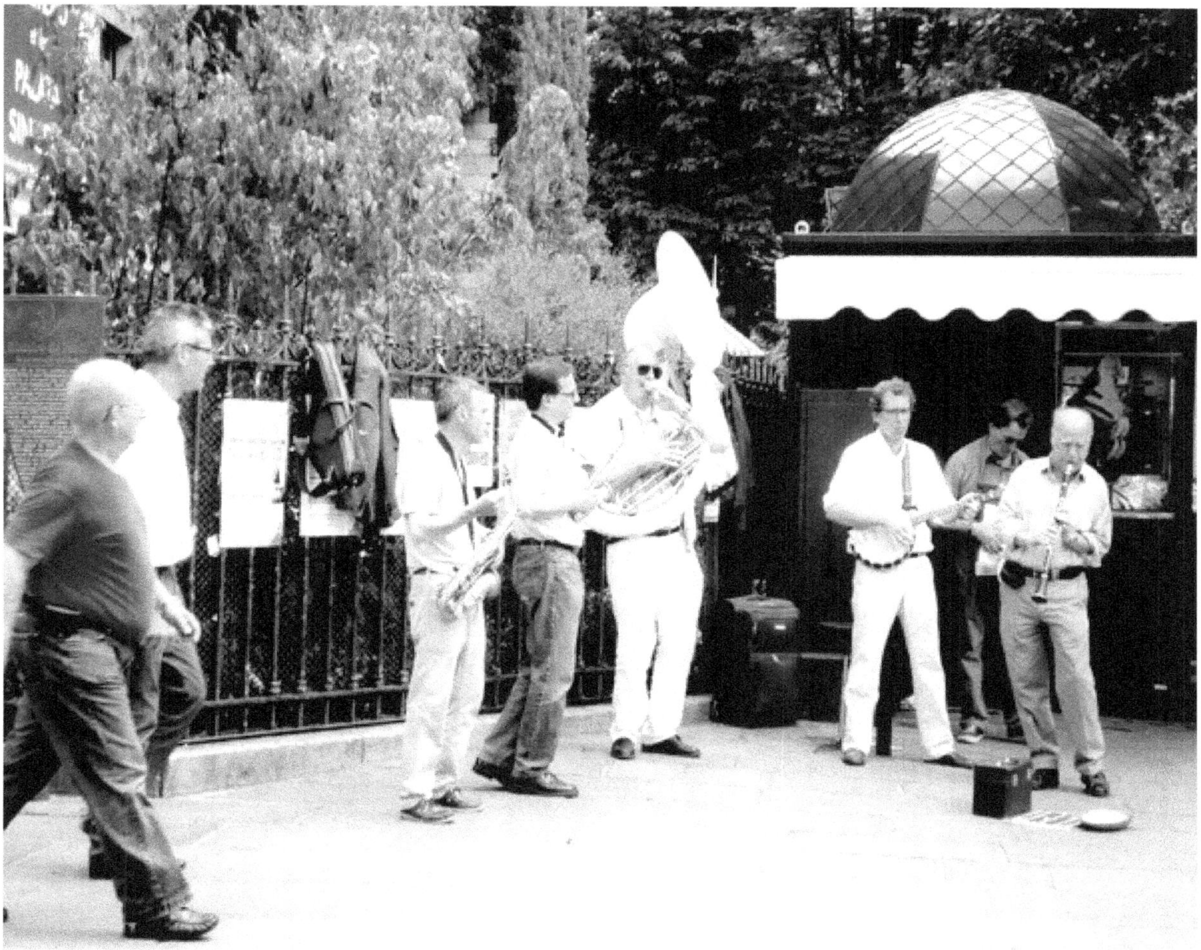

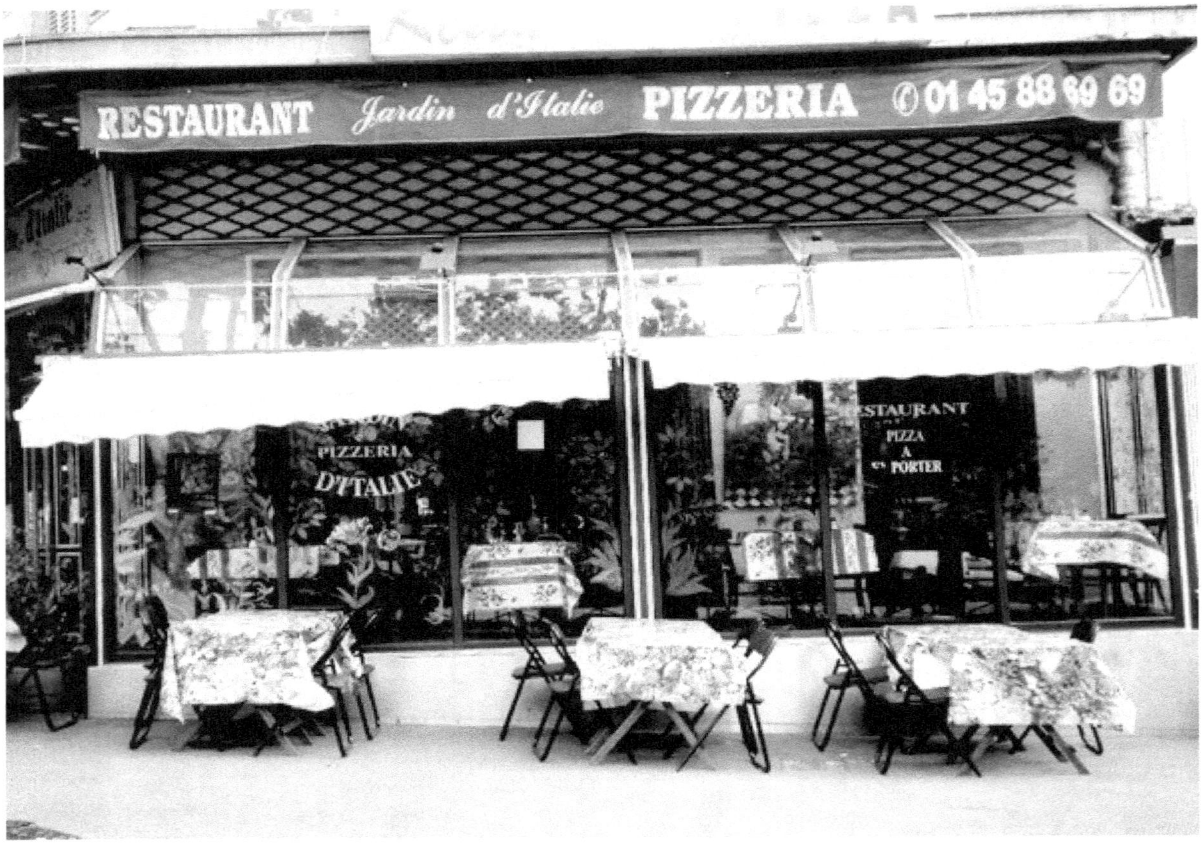
RESTAURANT Jardin d'Italie PIZZERIA
PIZZERIA
D'ITALIE
RESTAURANT
PIZZA
A
PORTER

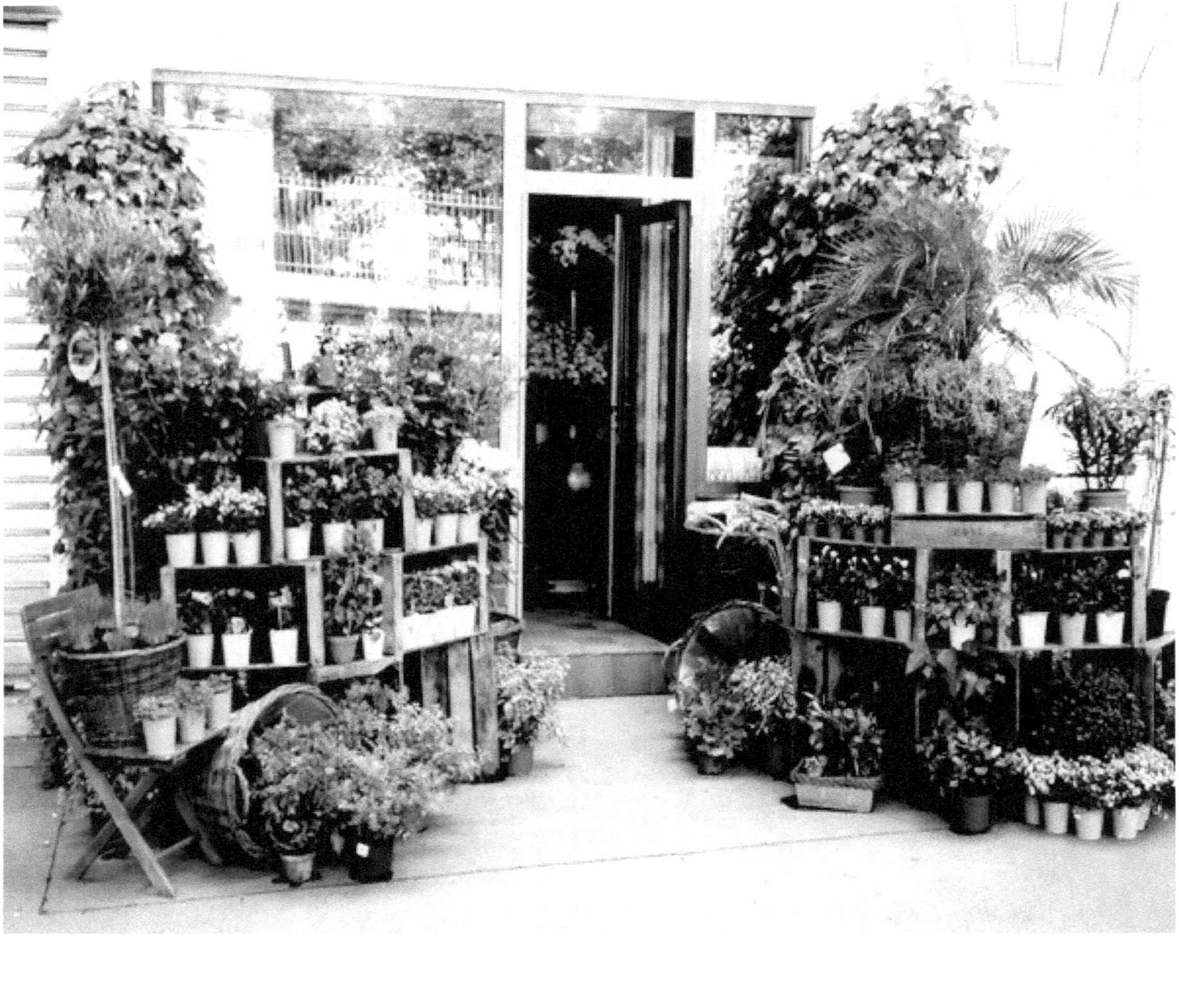

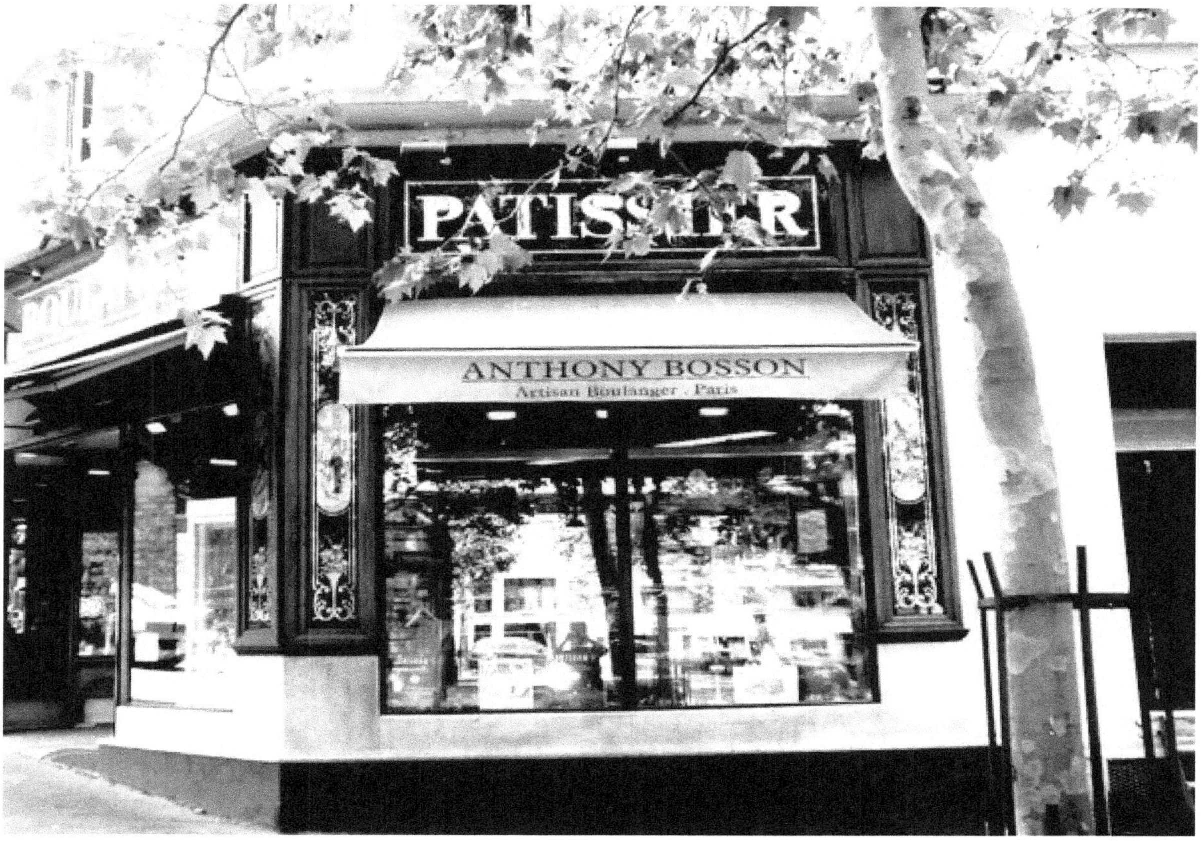
PATISSIER
ANTHONY BOSSON
Artisan Boulanger . Paris

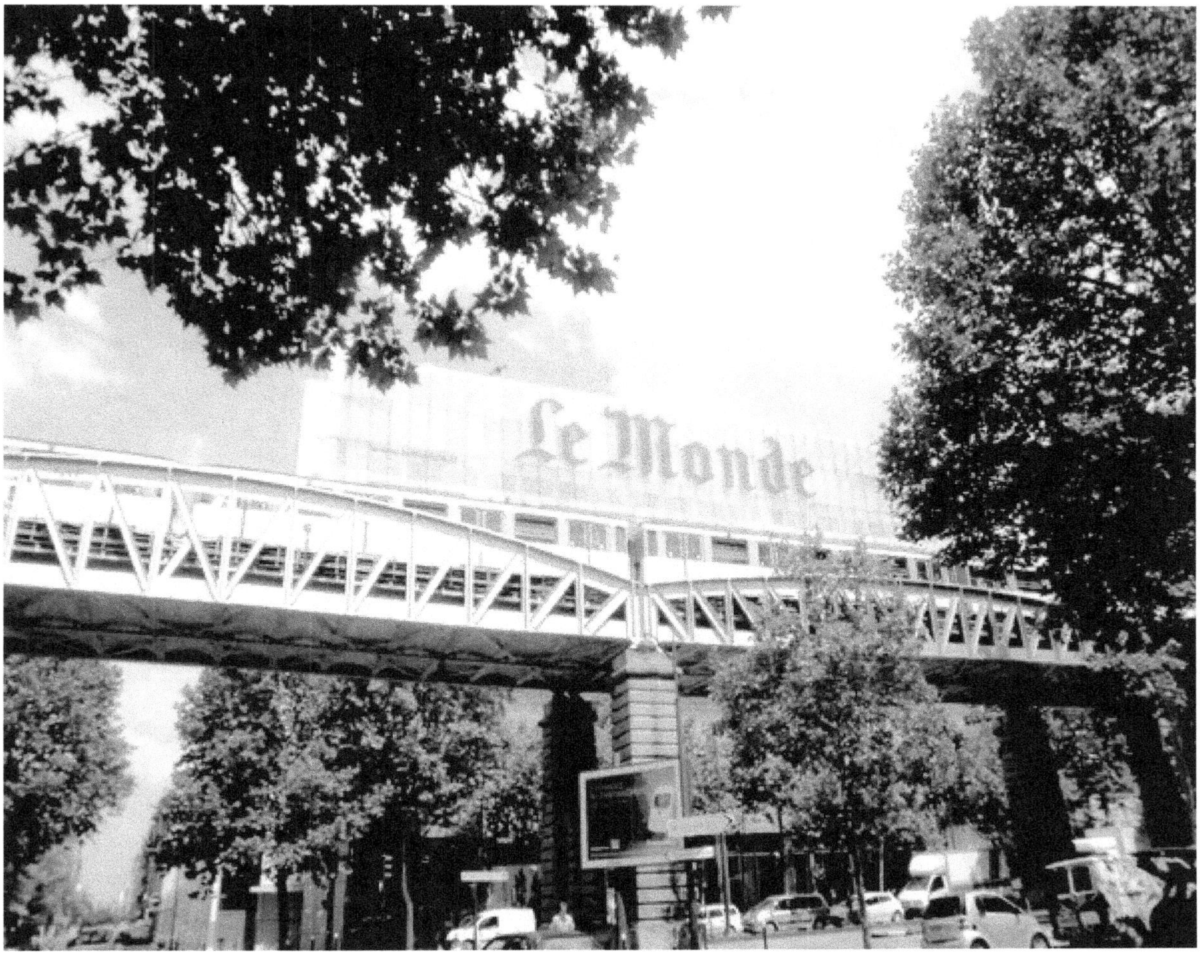
Le Monde

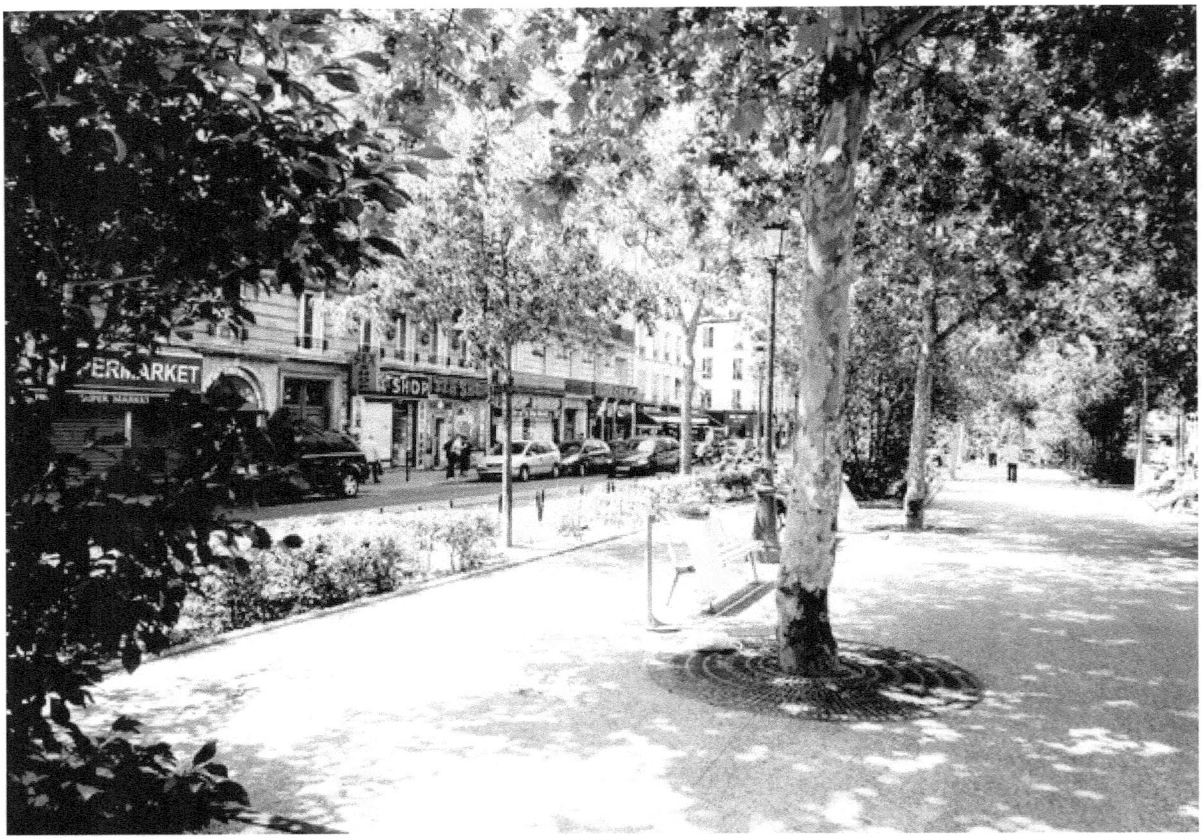
PERMARKET
SHOP

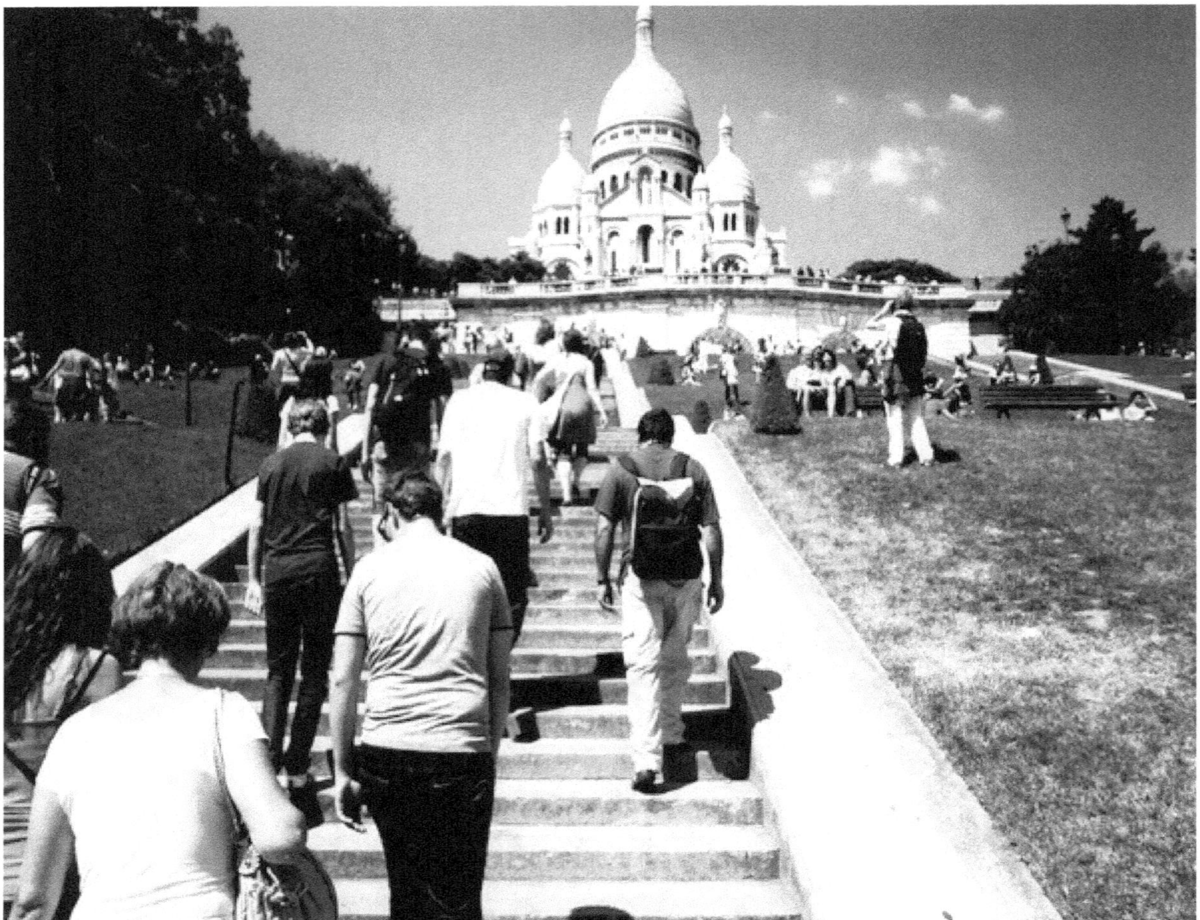

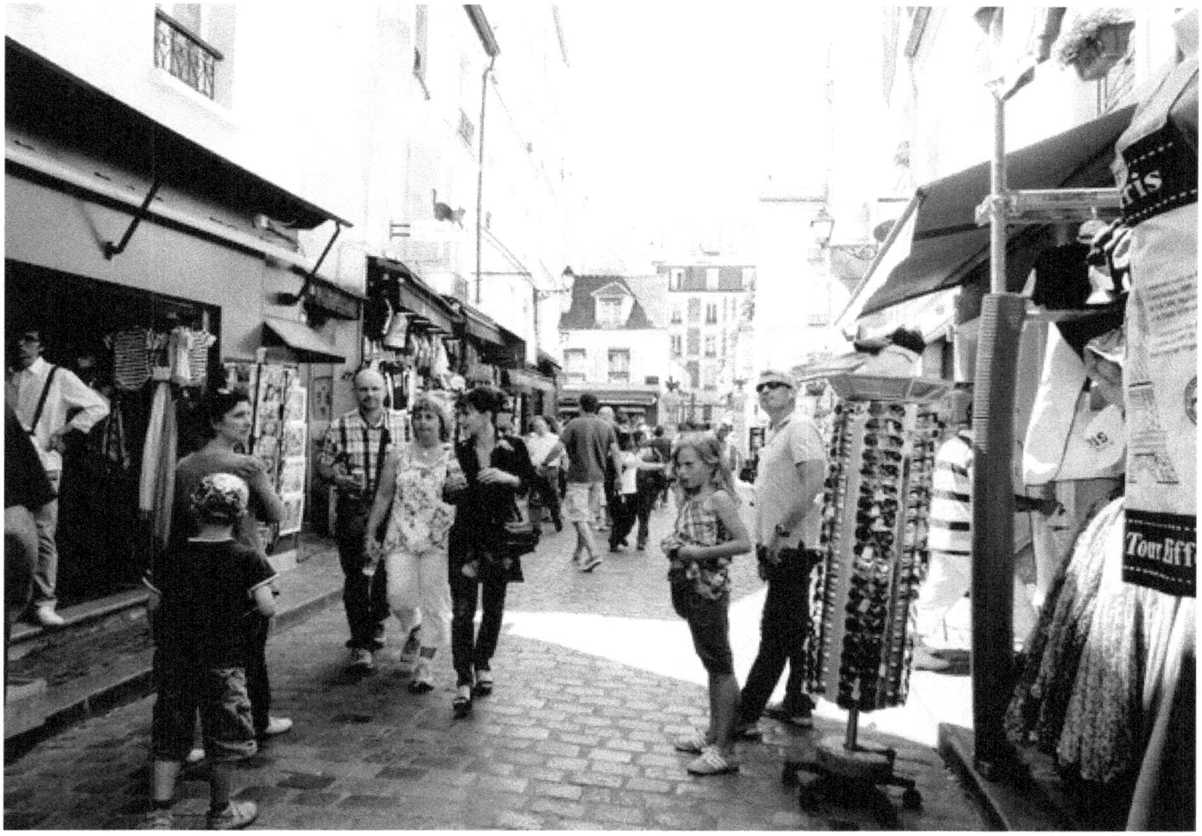

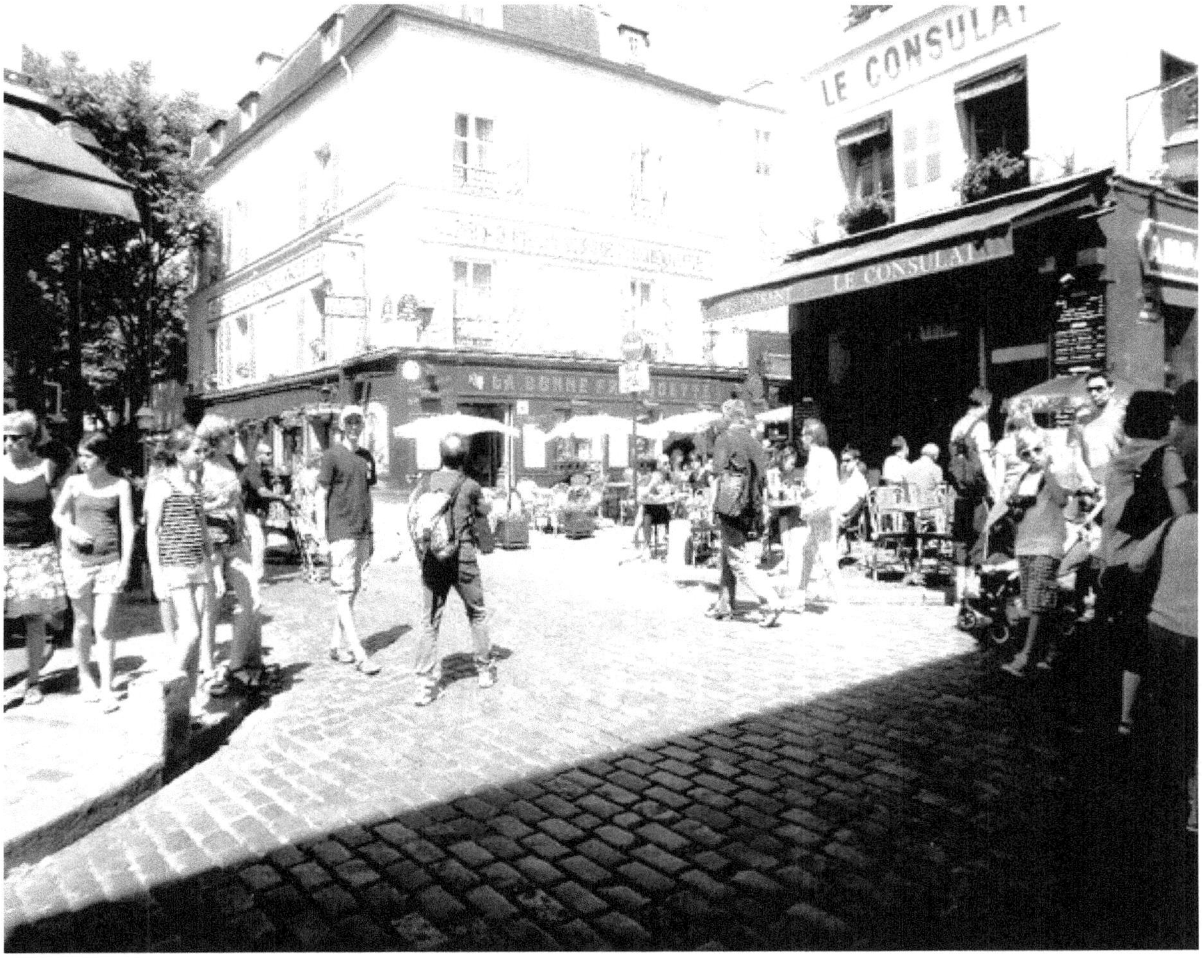
LE CONSULAT

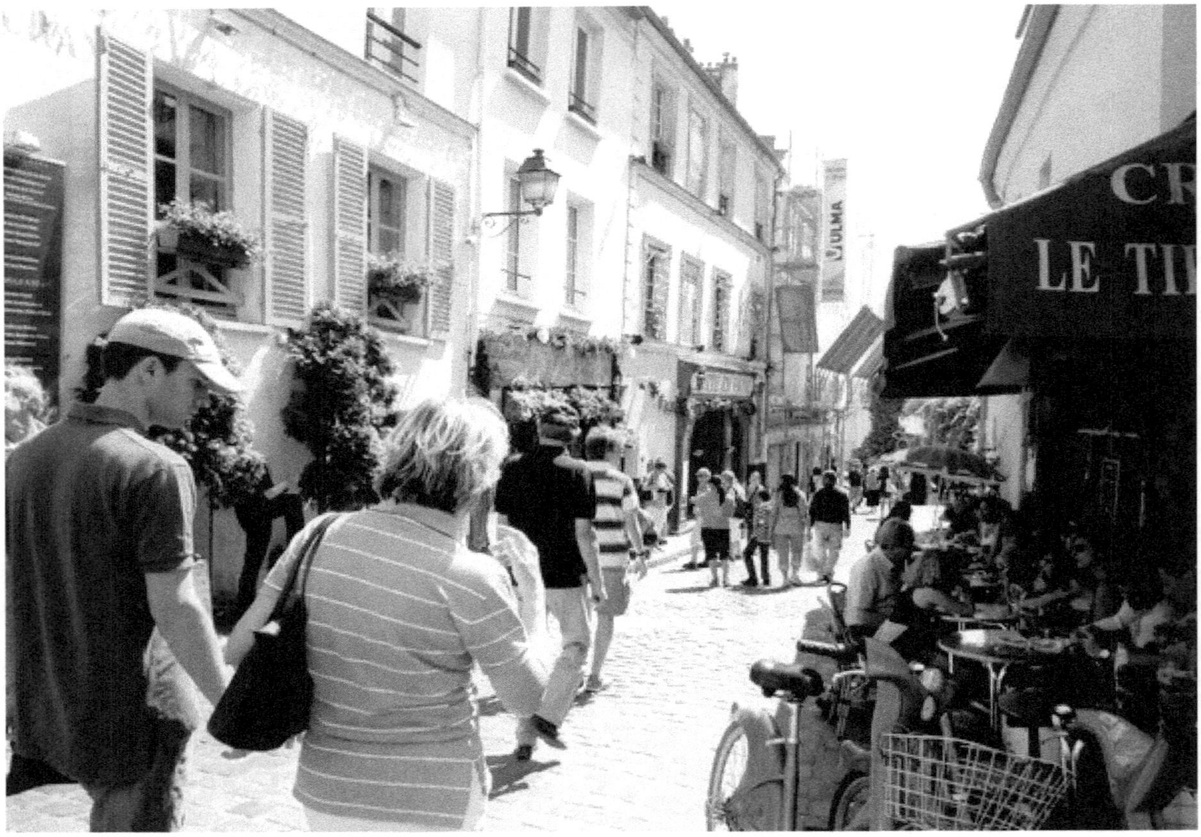
CR
LE TI

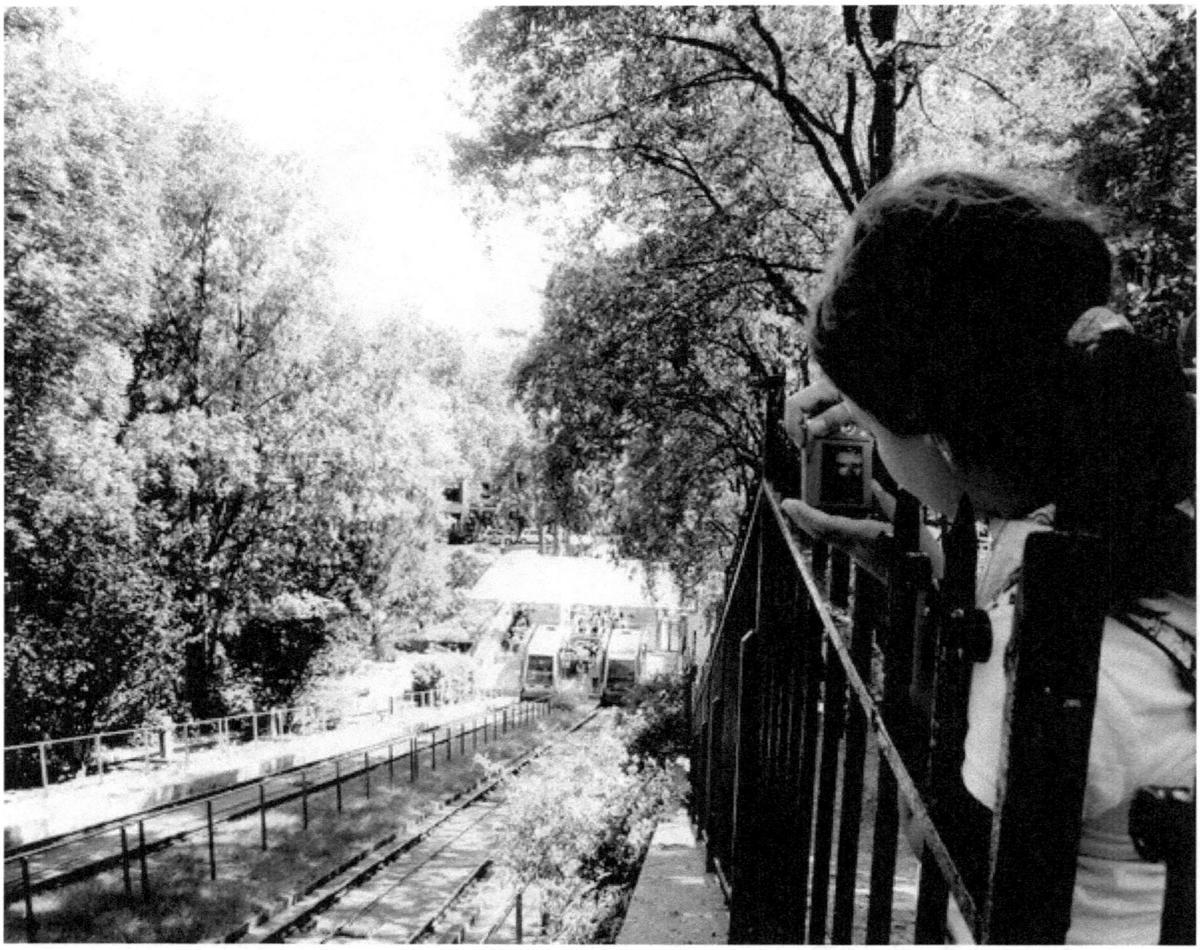

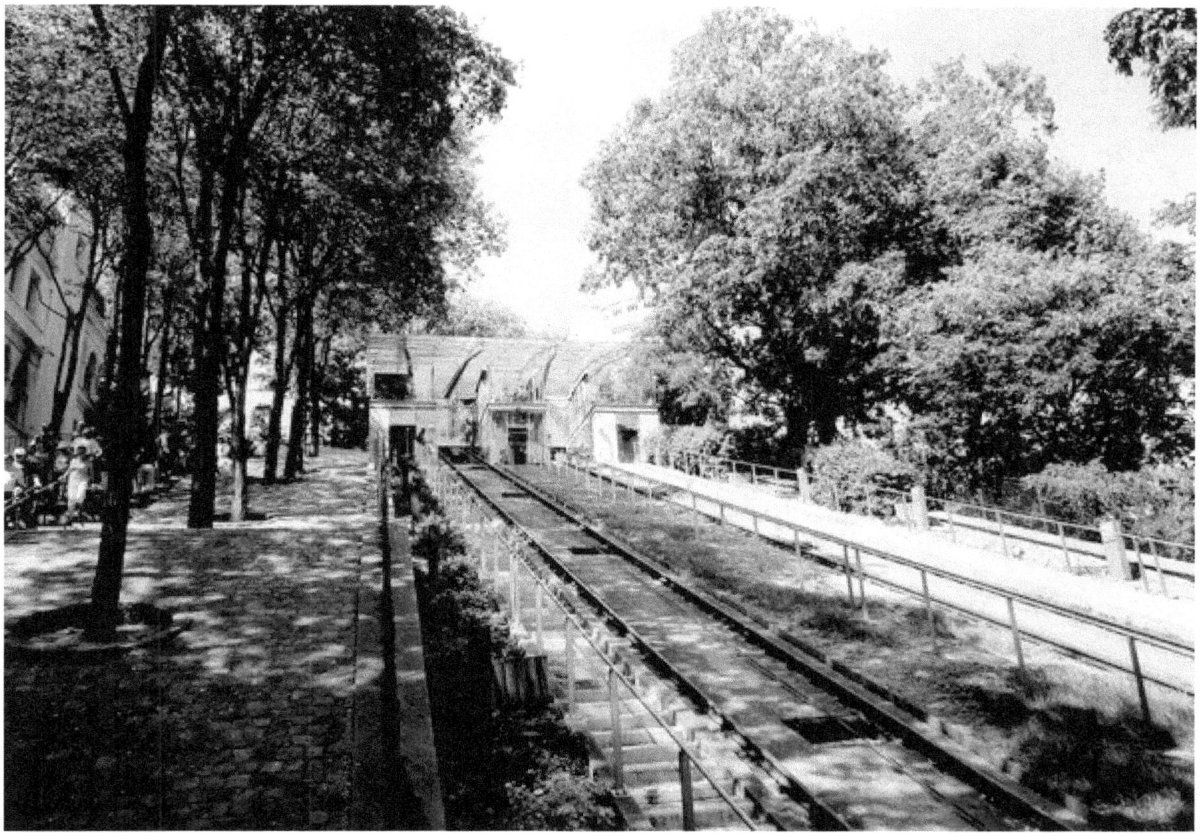

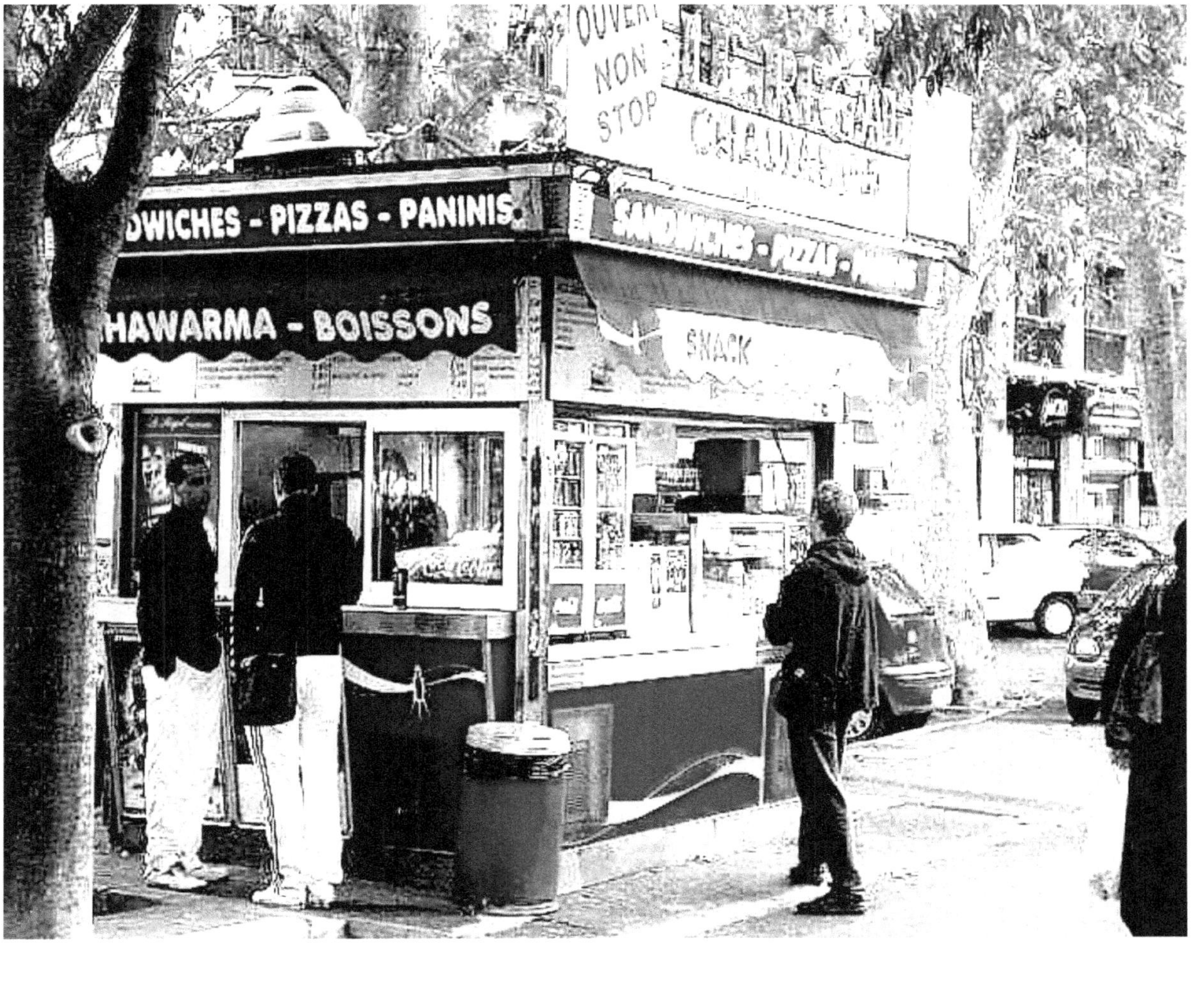
OUVERT
NON
STOP
DWICHES - PIZZAS - PANINIS
HAWARMA - BOISSONS
SNACK

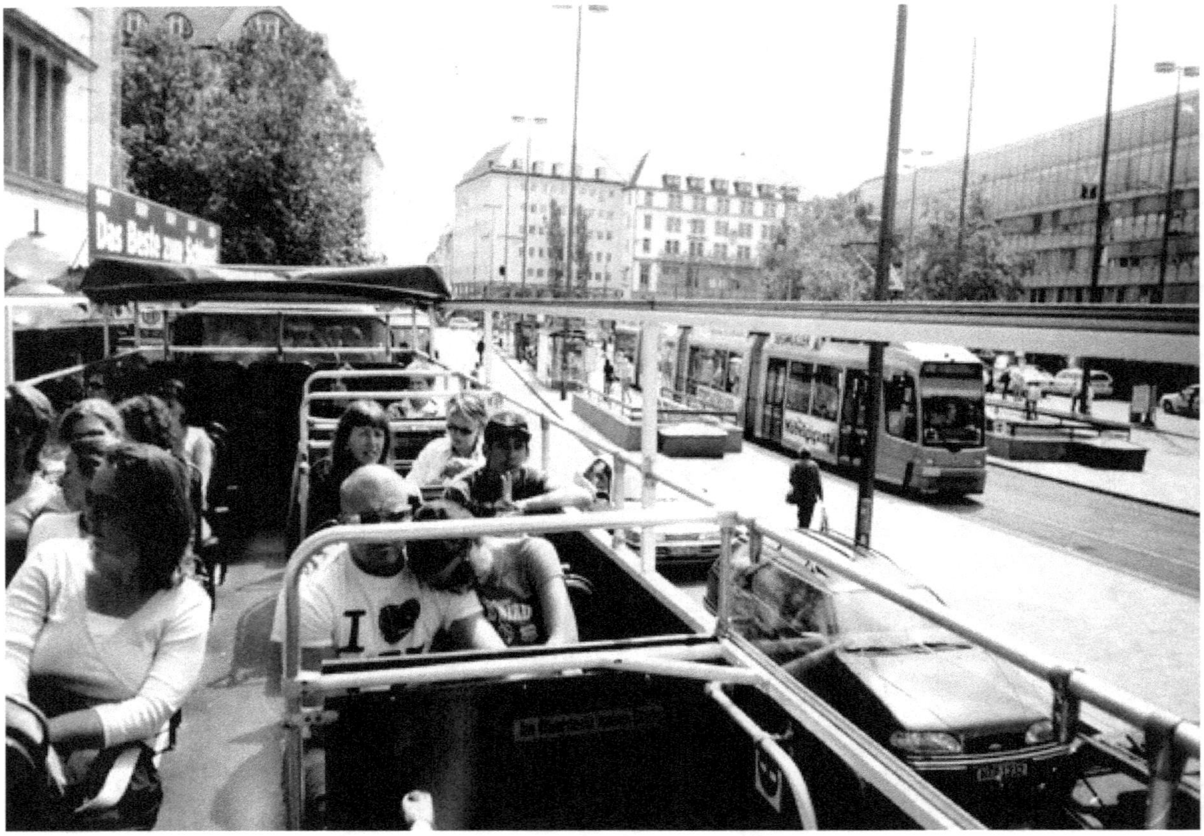

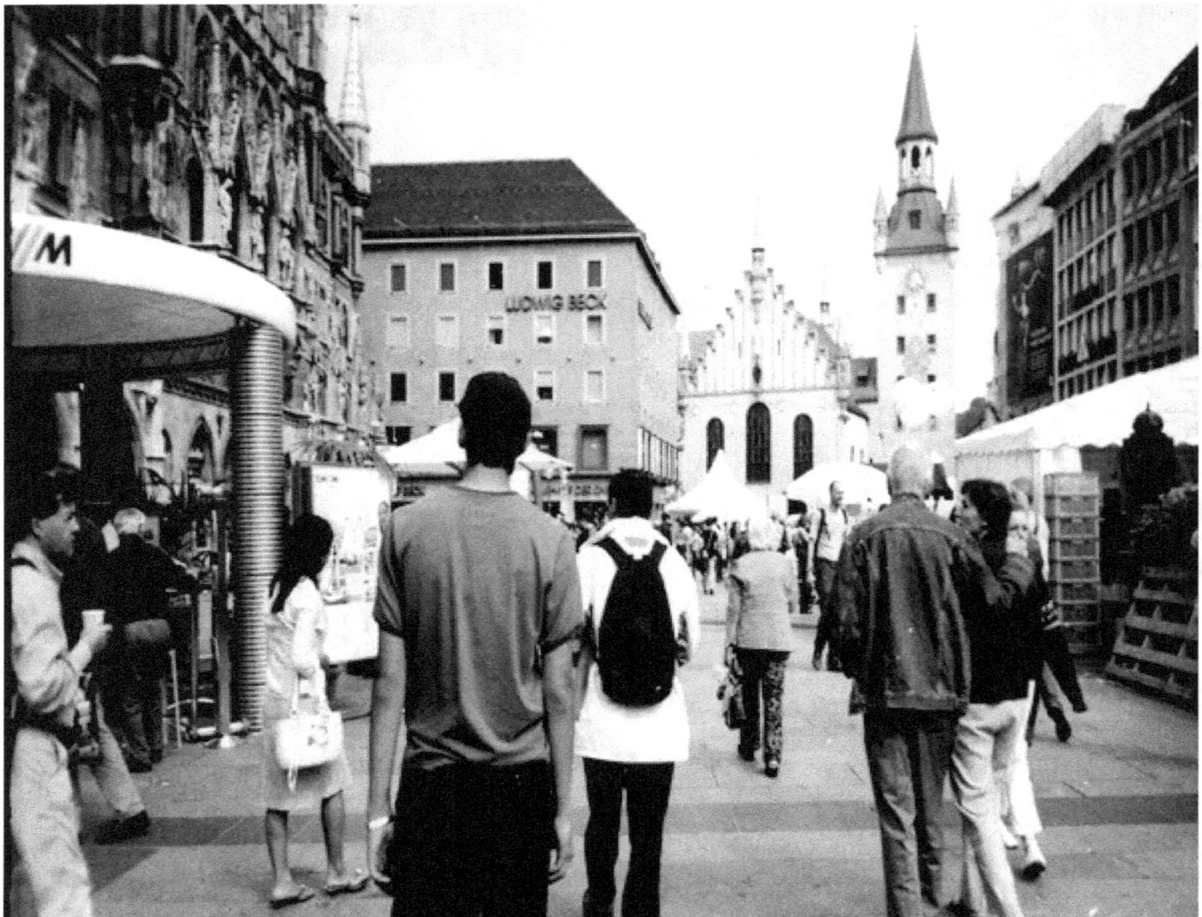
LUDWIG BECK

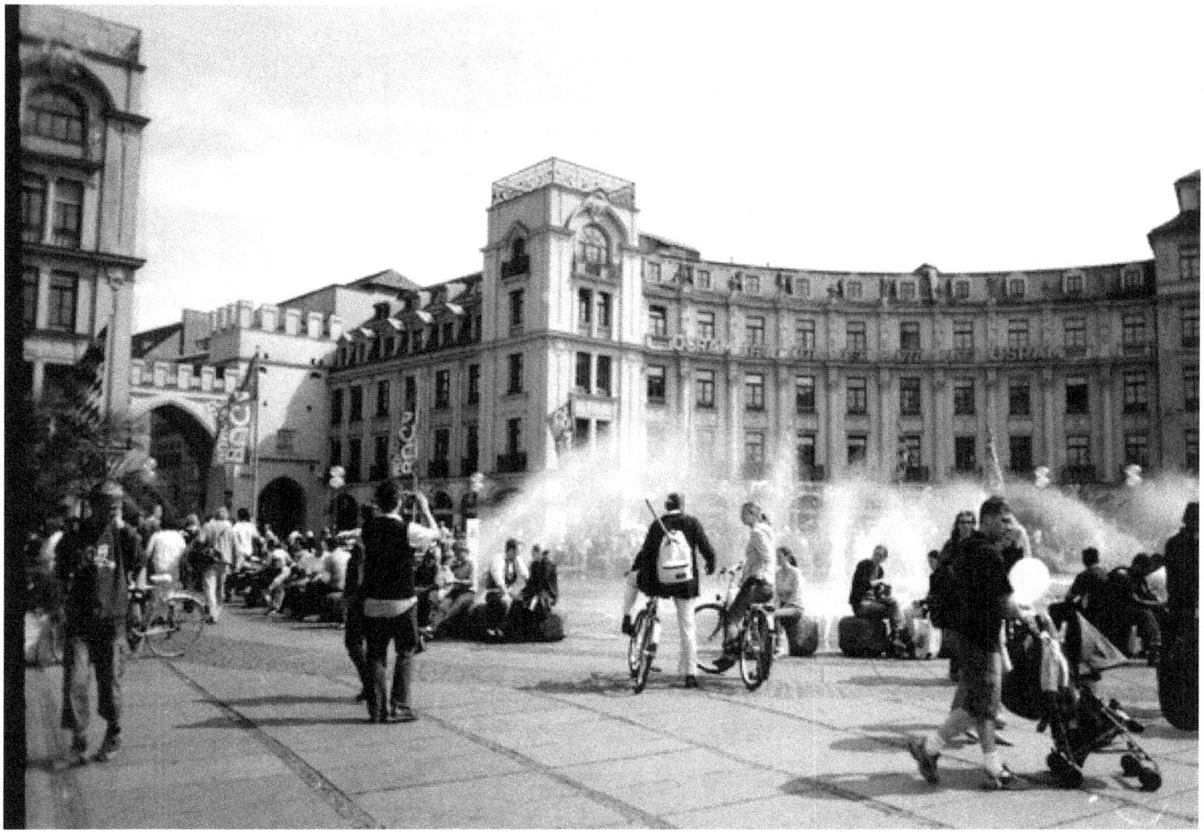

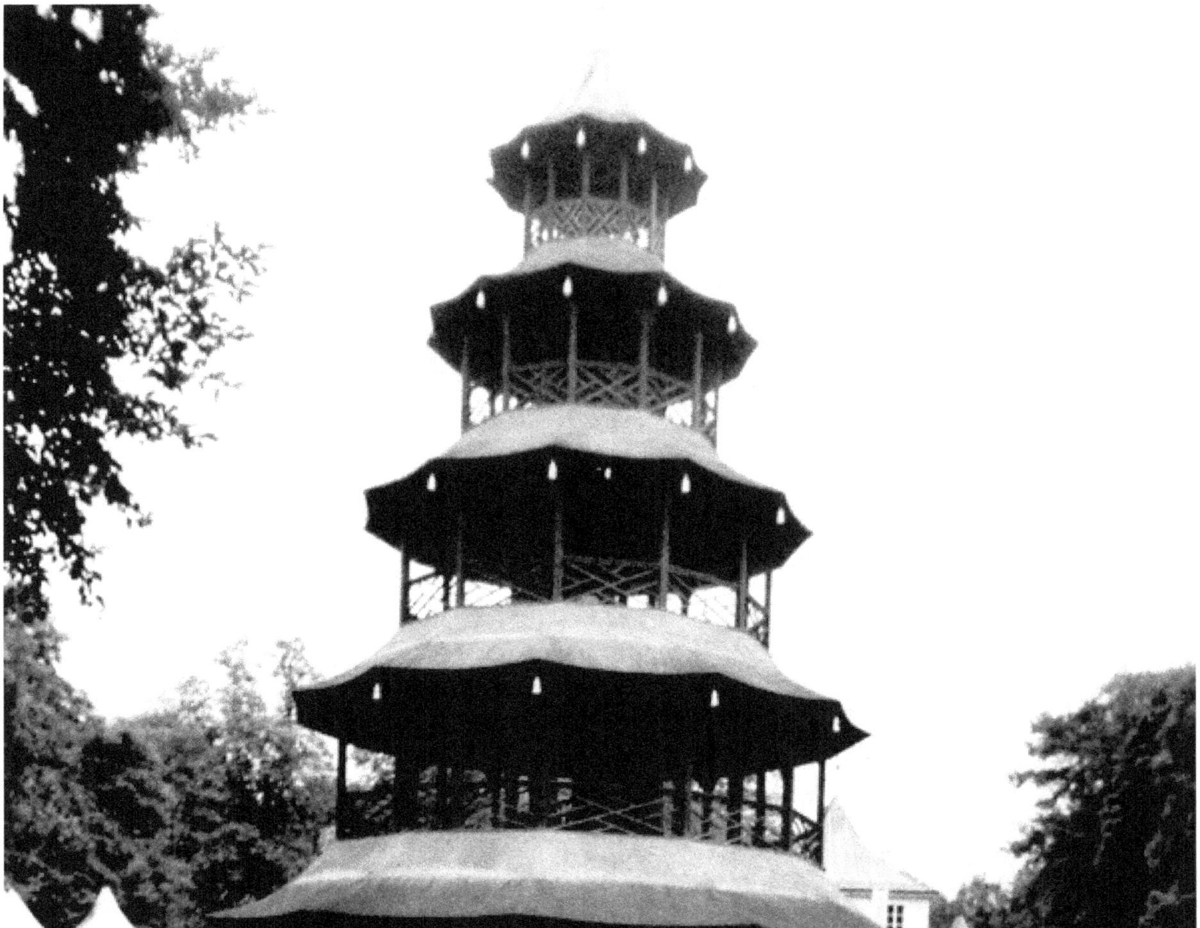

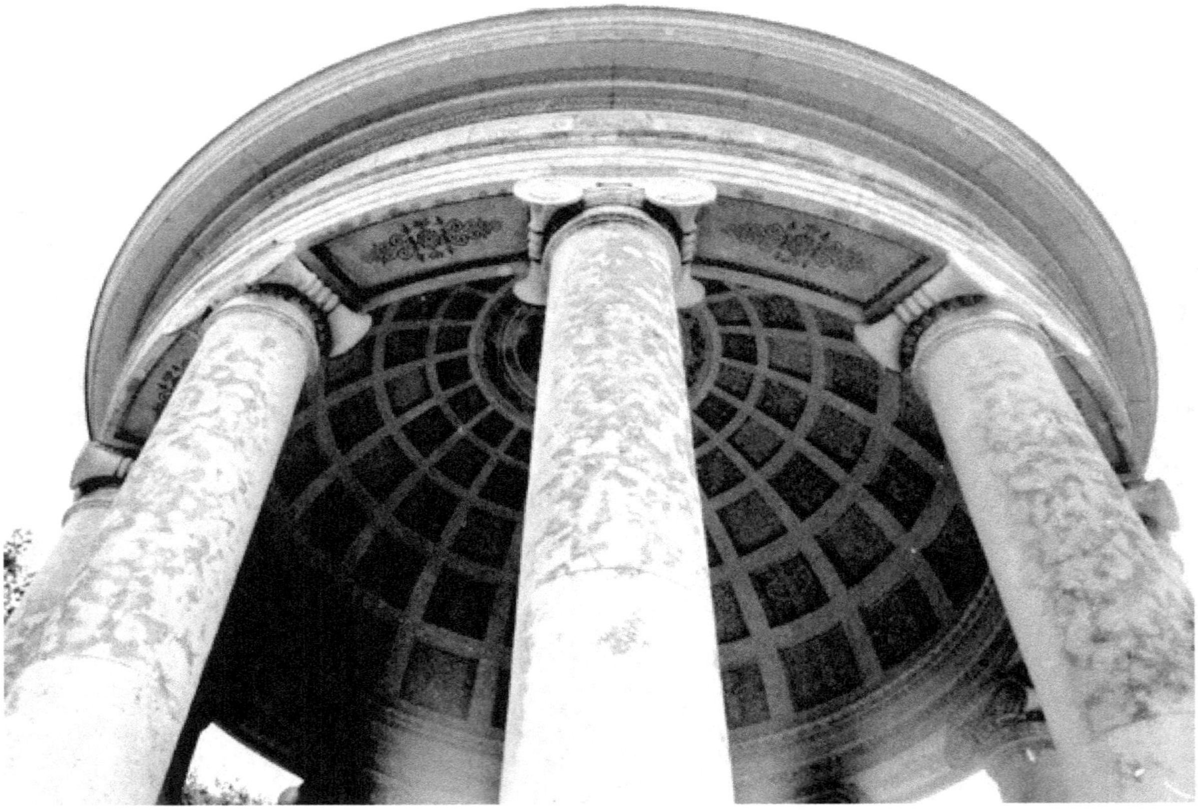

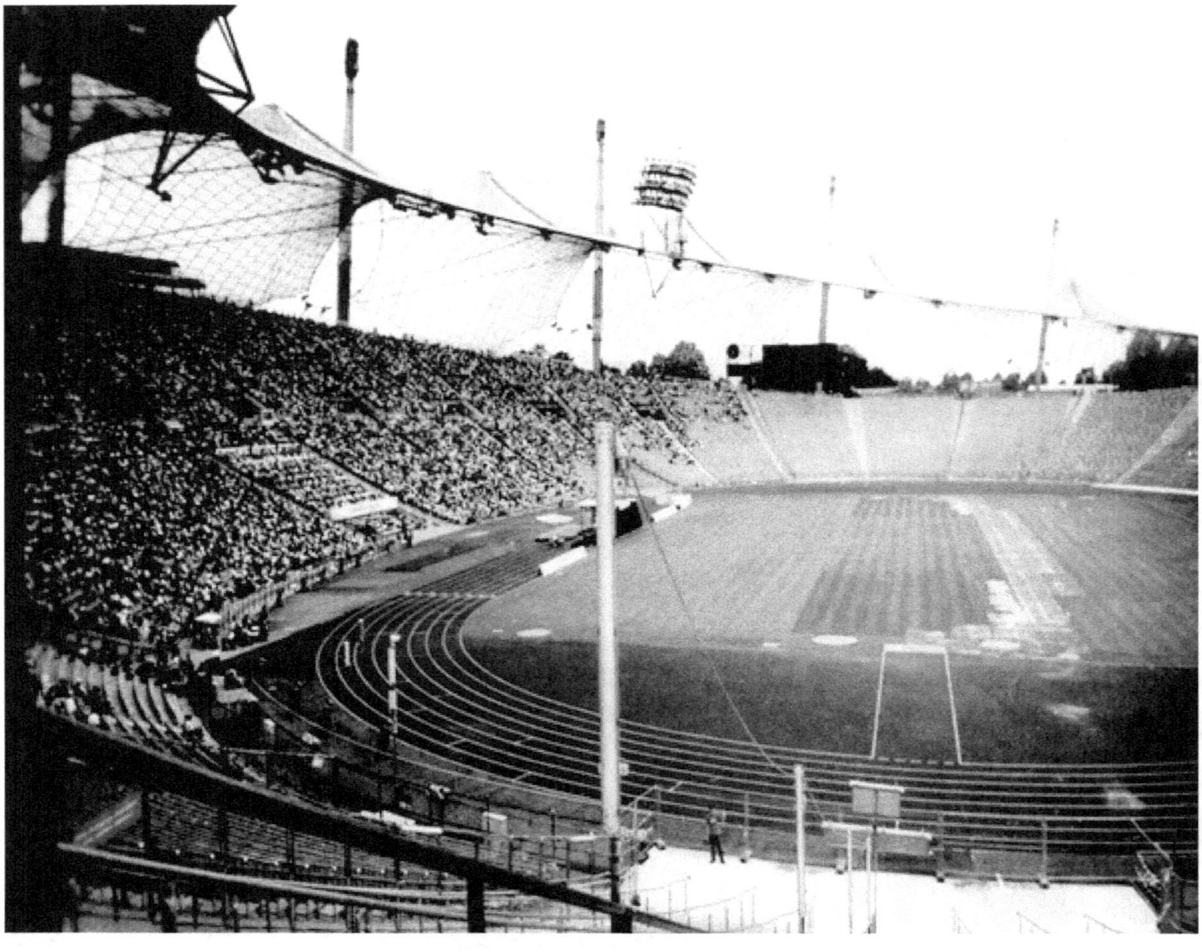

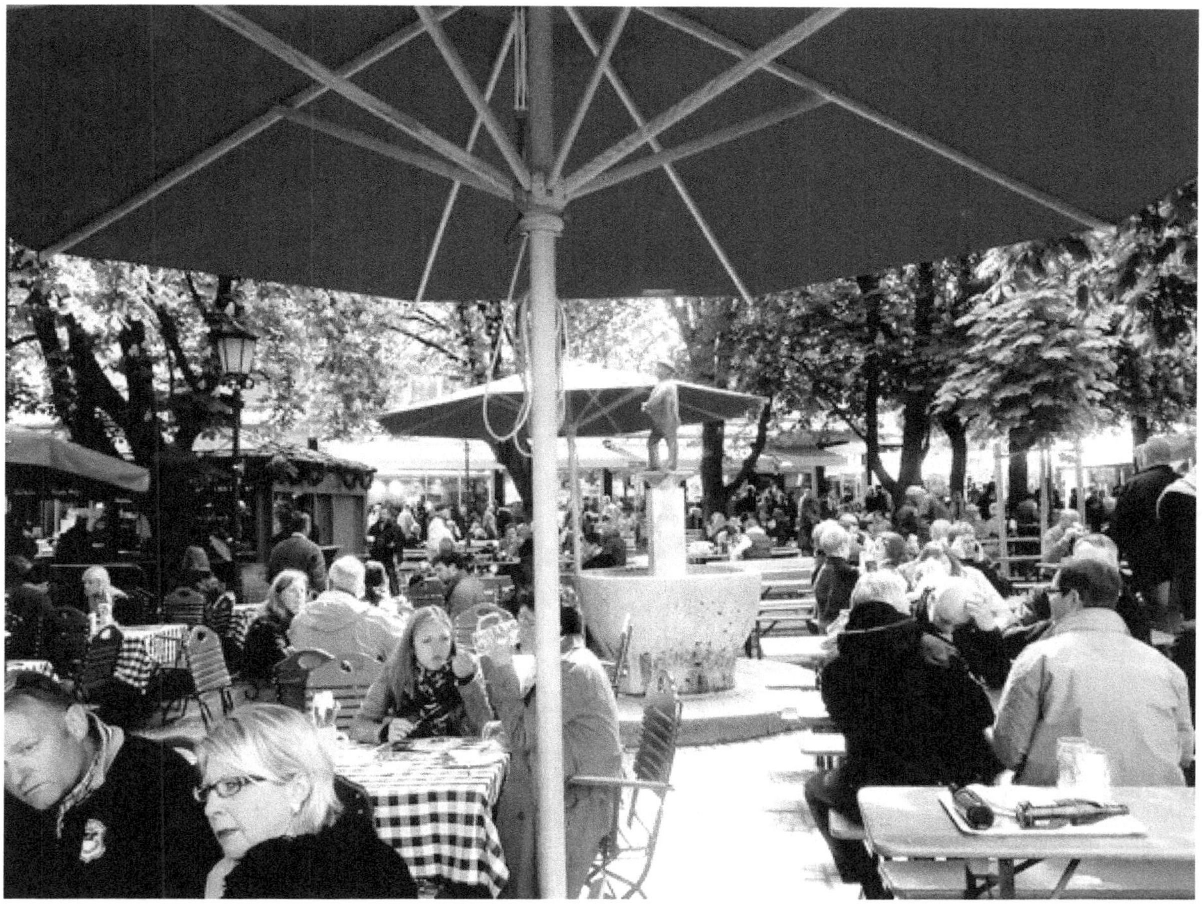

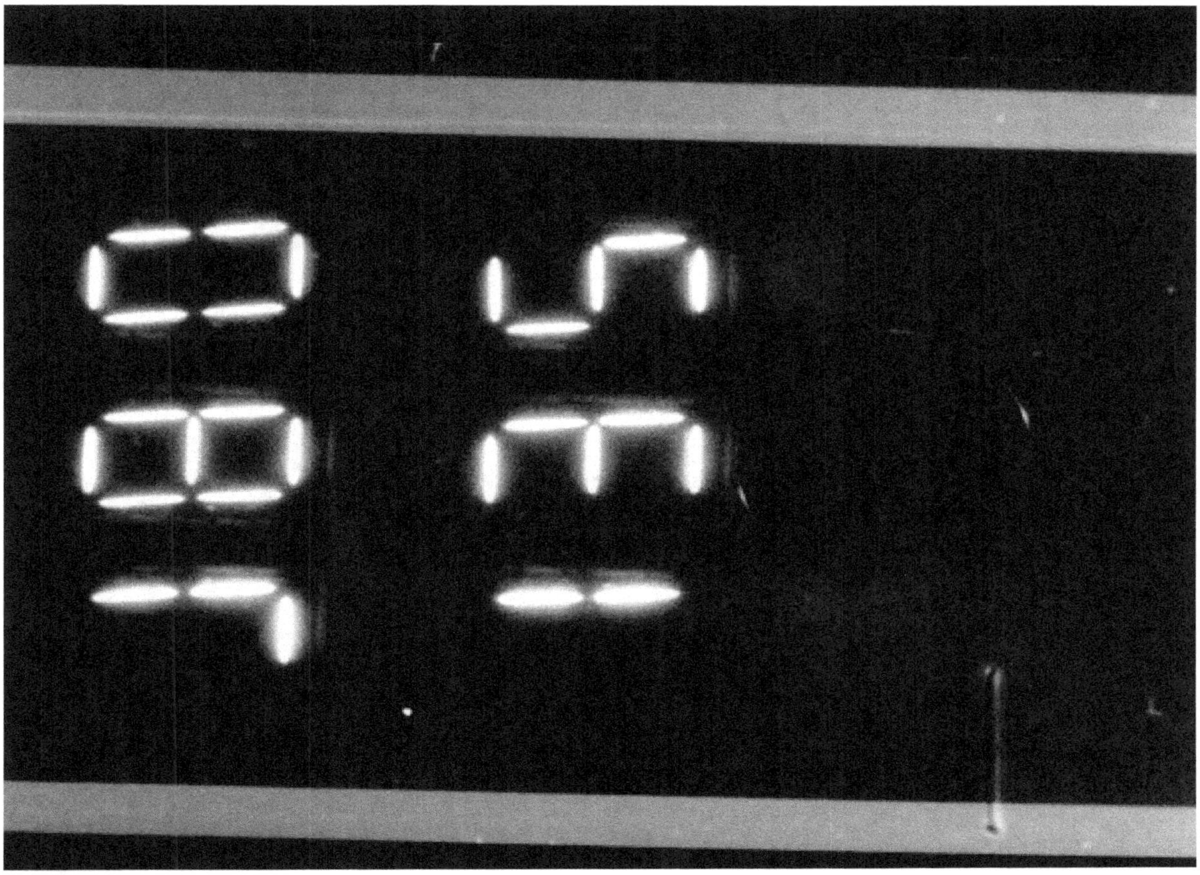

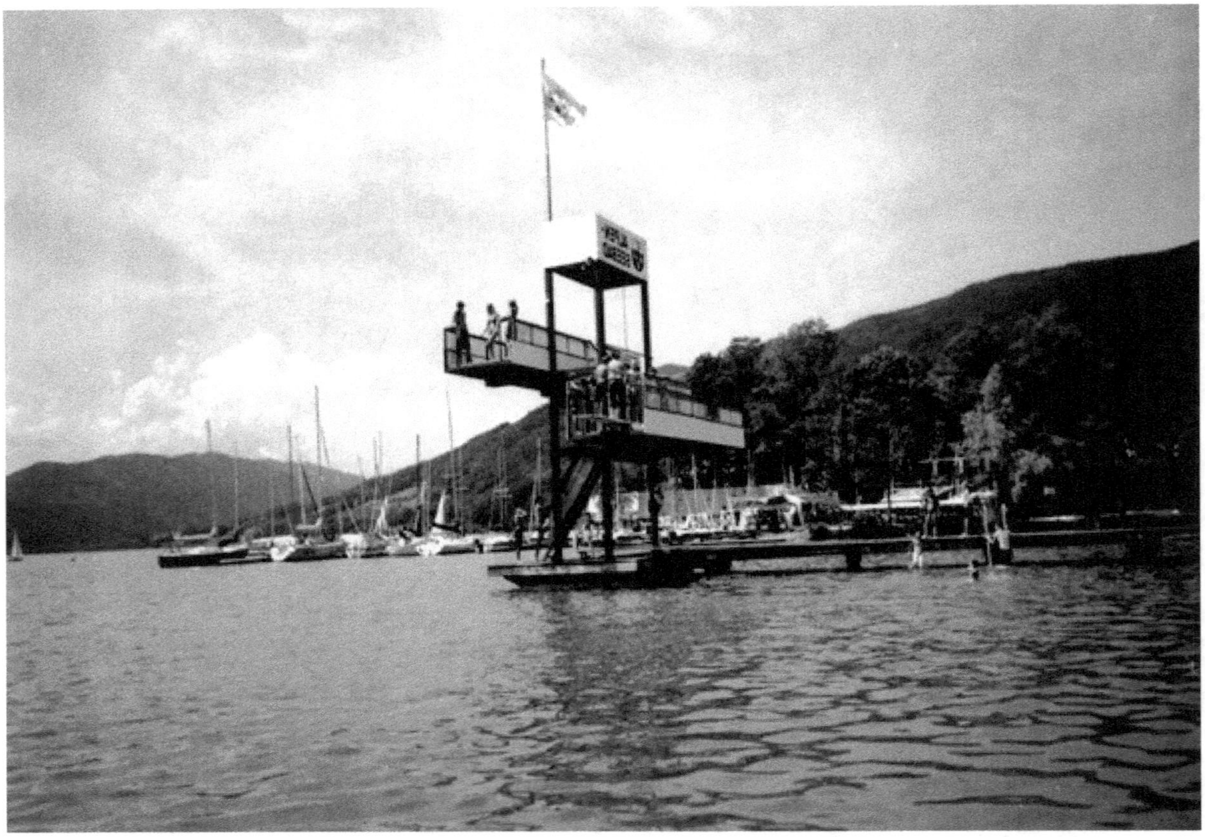

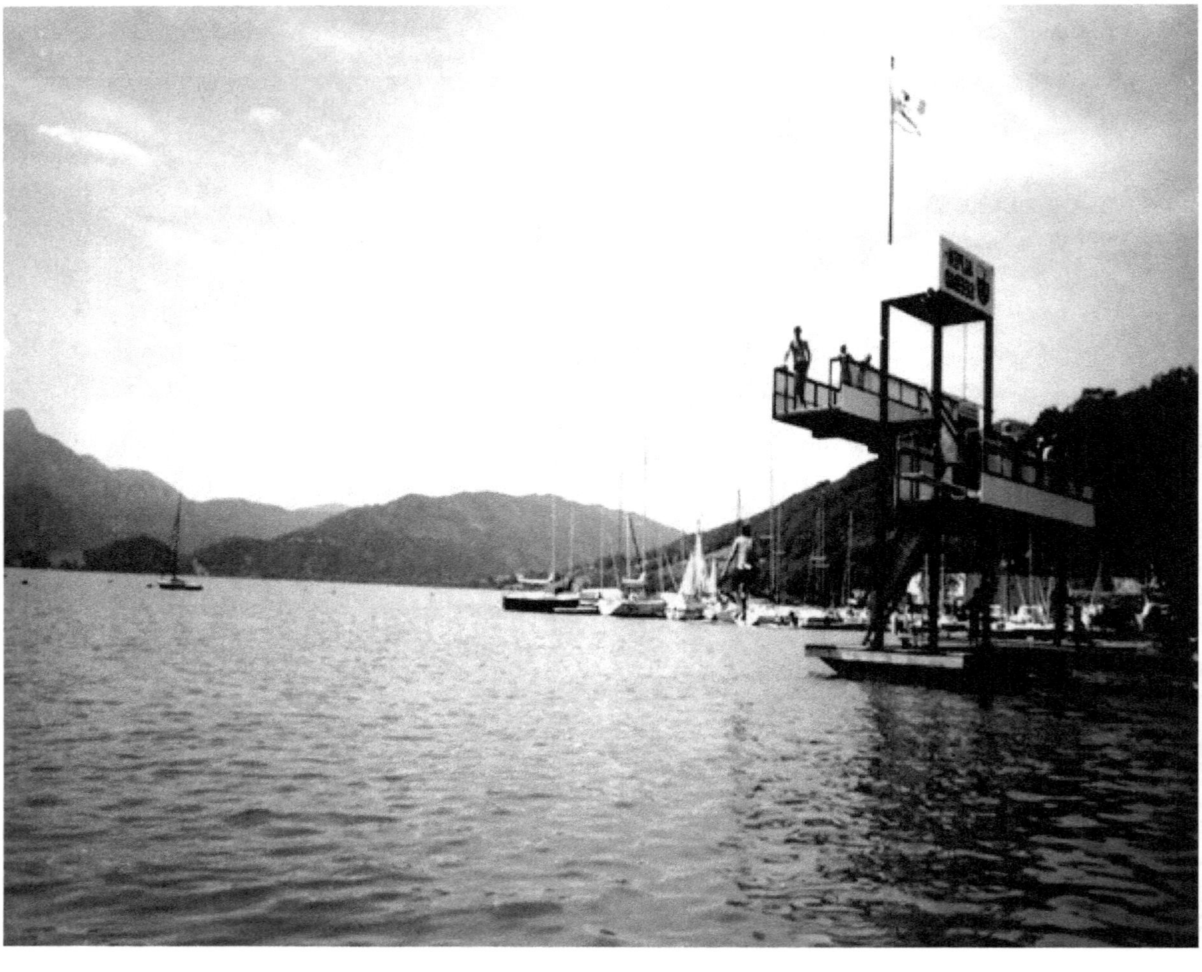

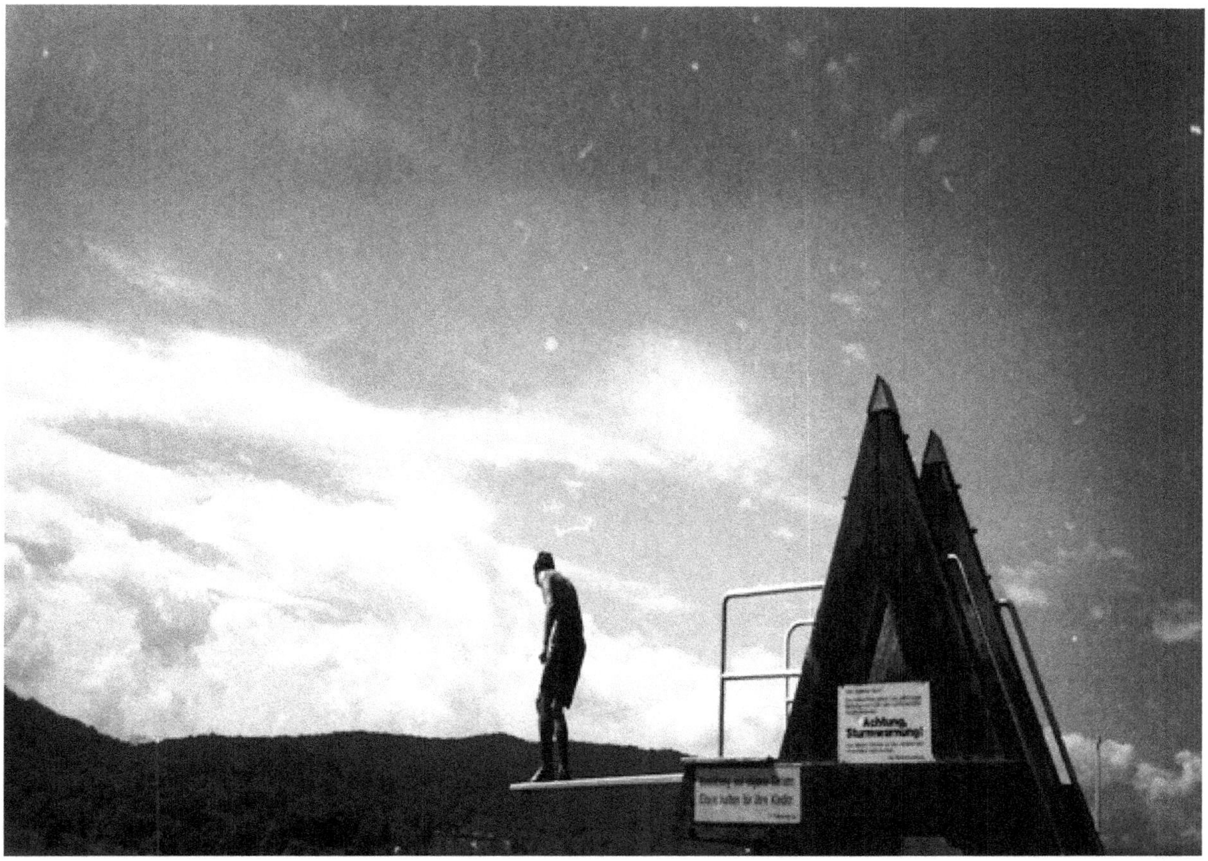
Achtung,
Sturmwarnung!

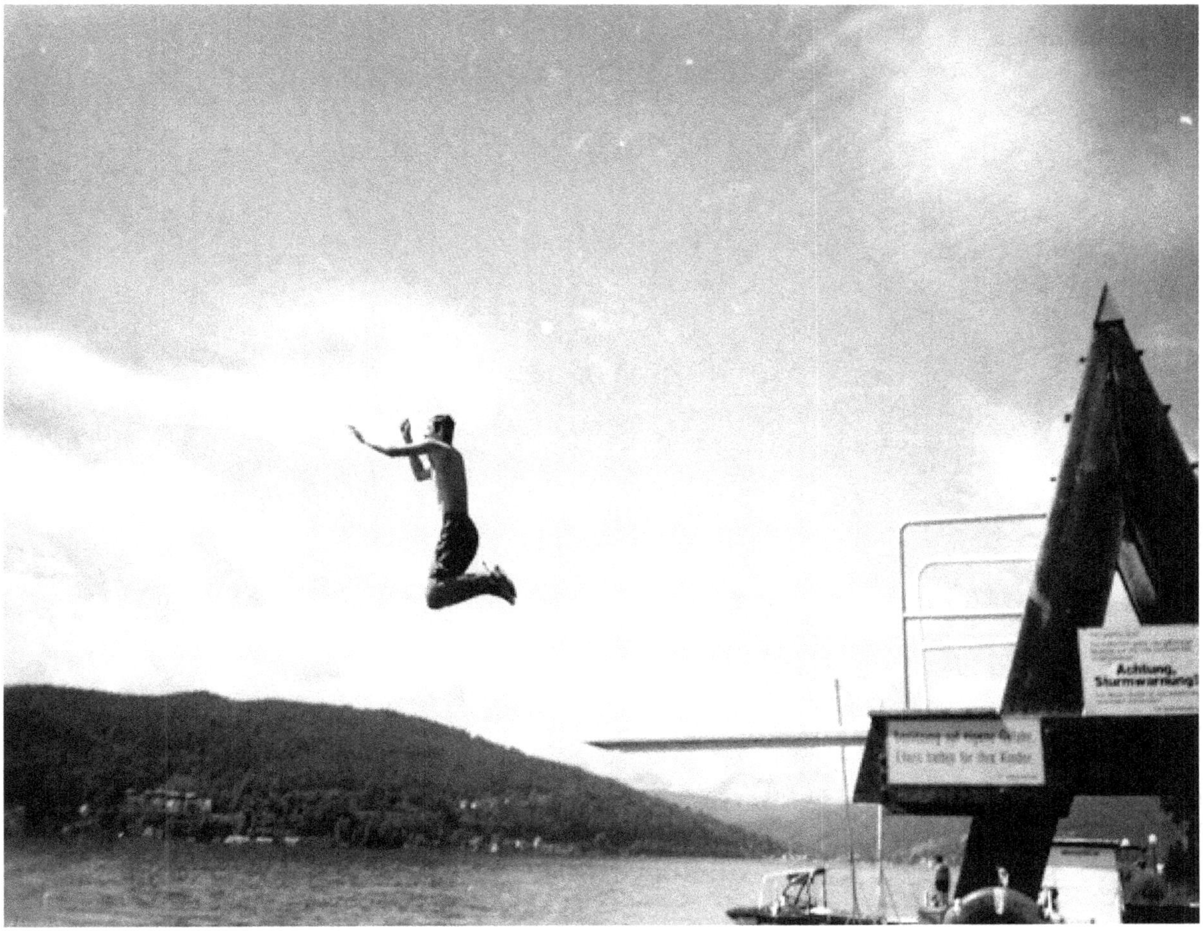
Achtung,
Sturmwarnung!

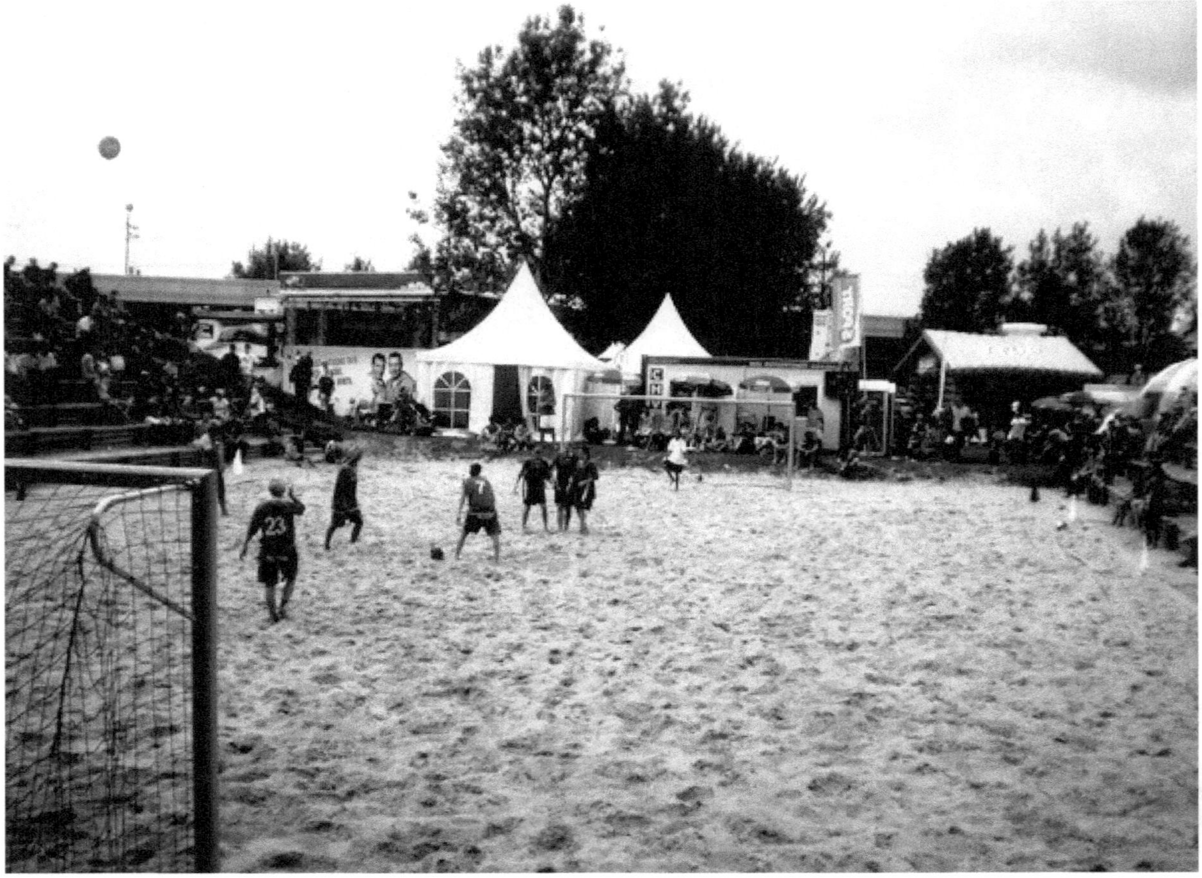

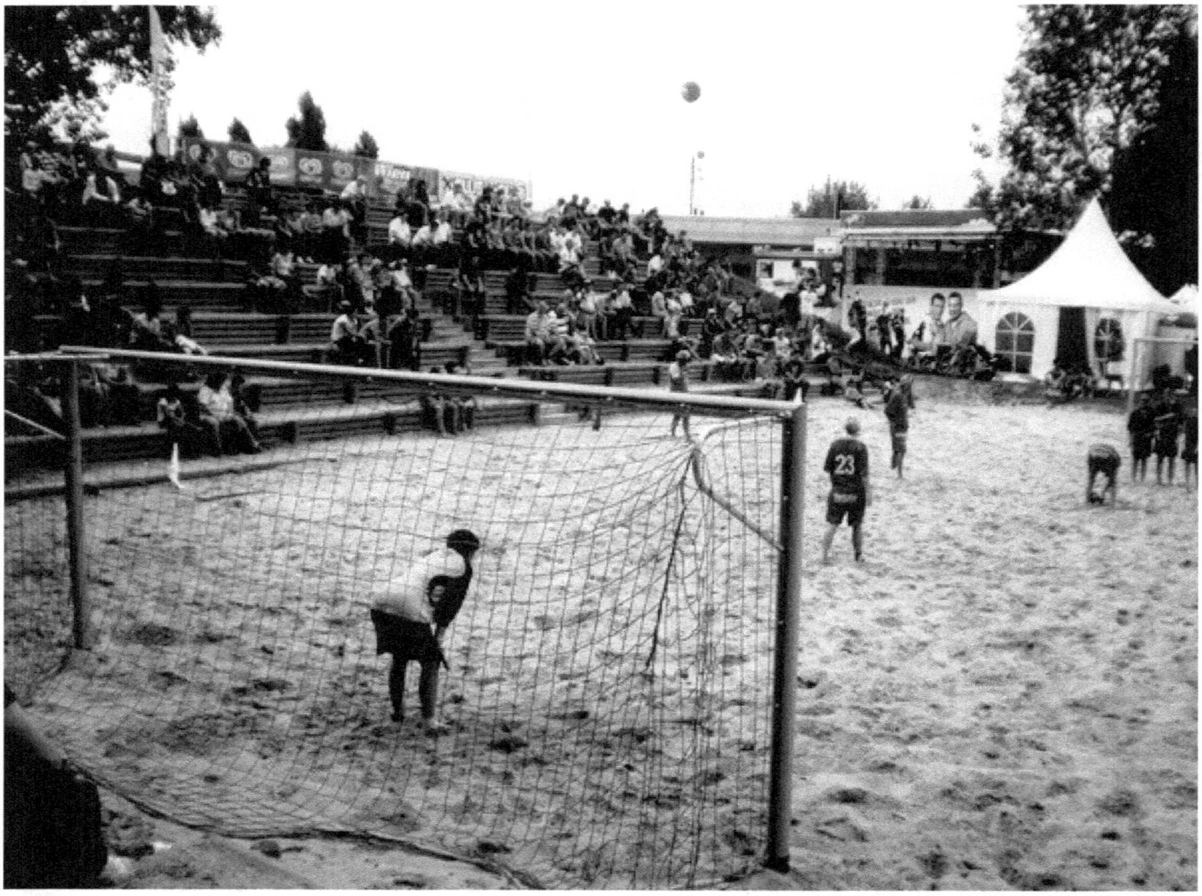

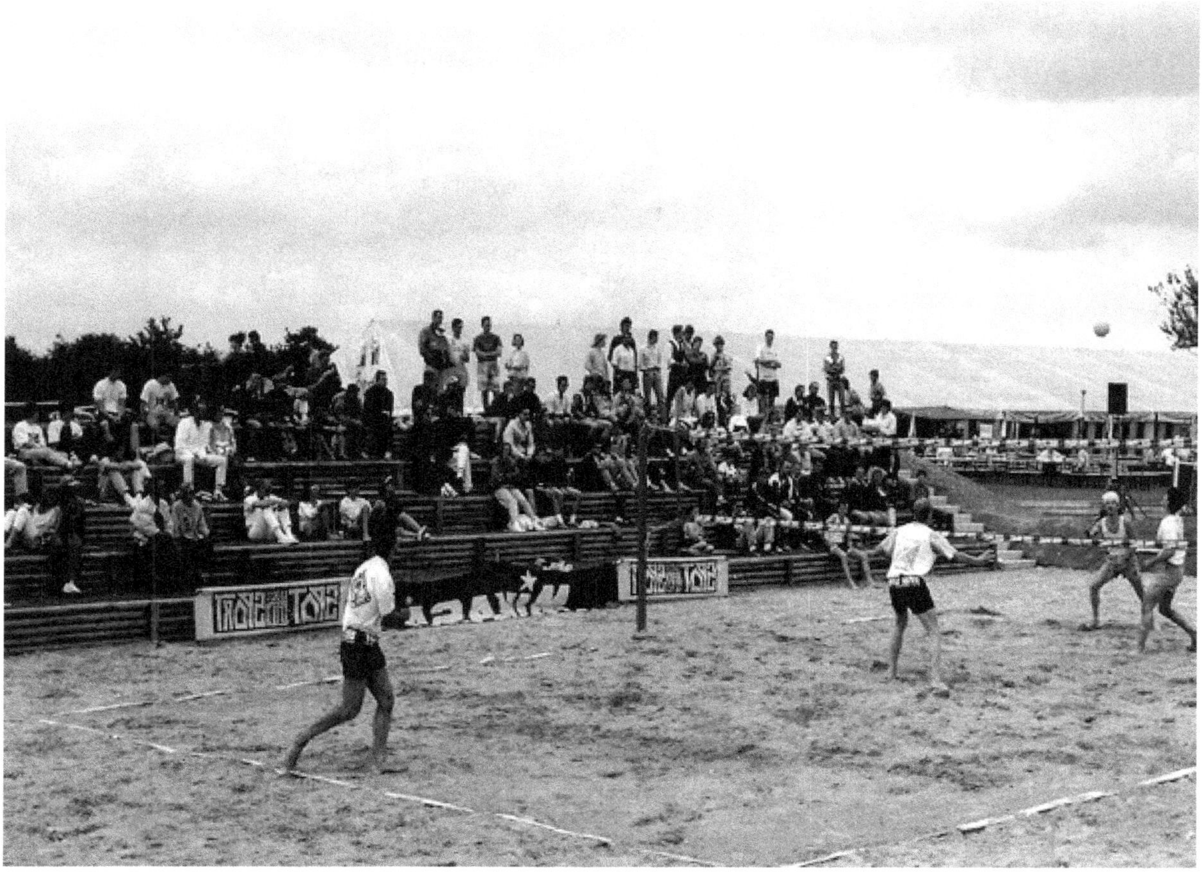

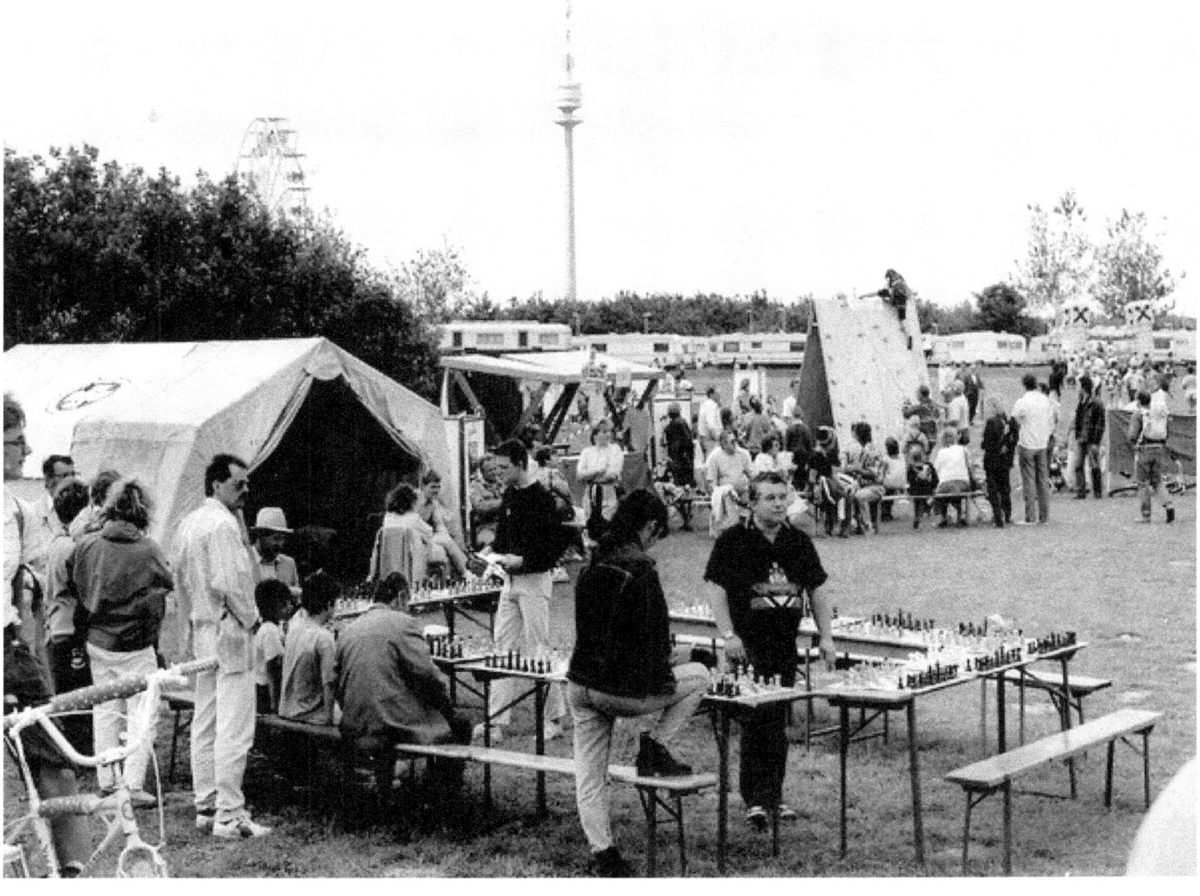

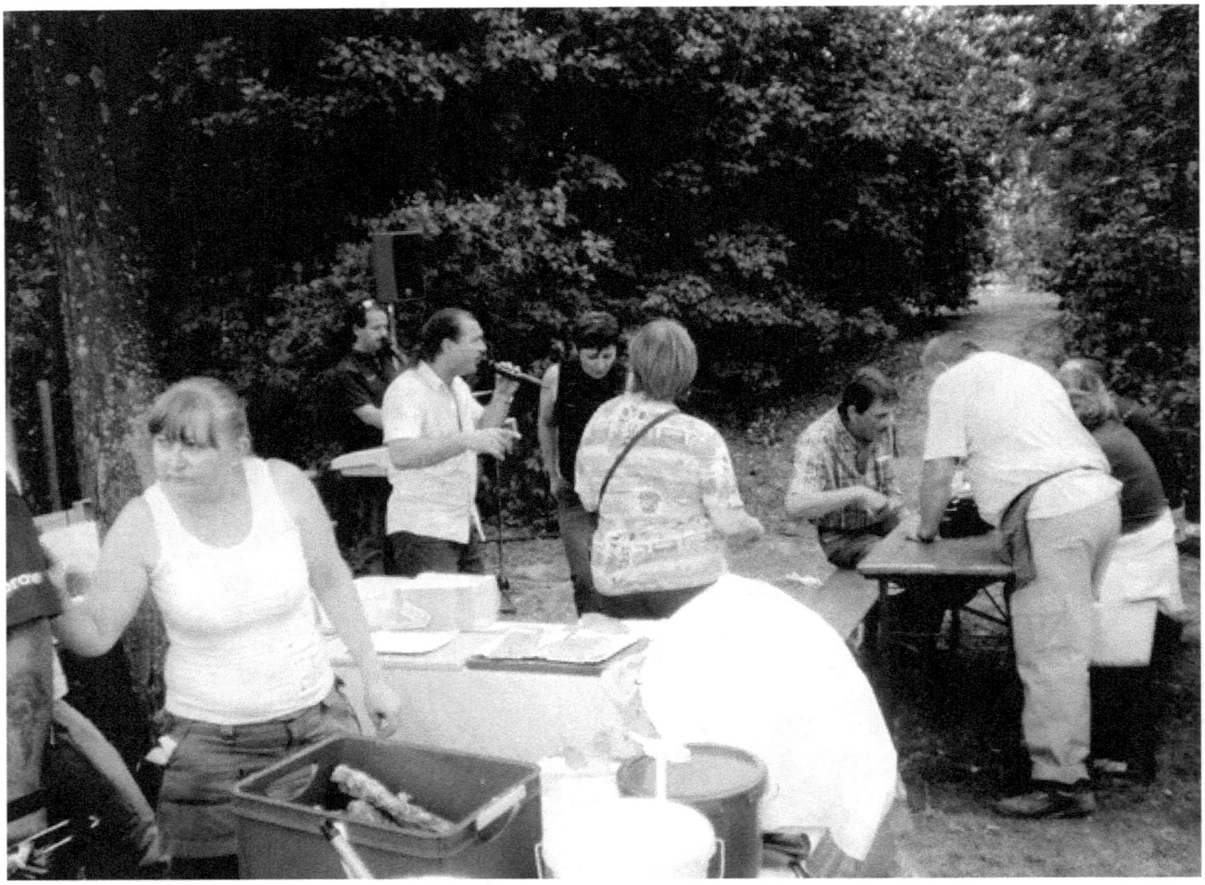

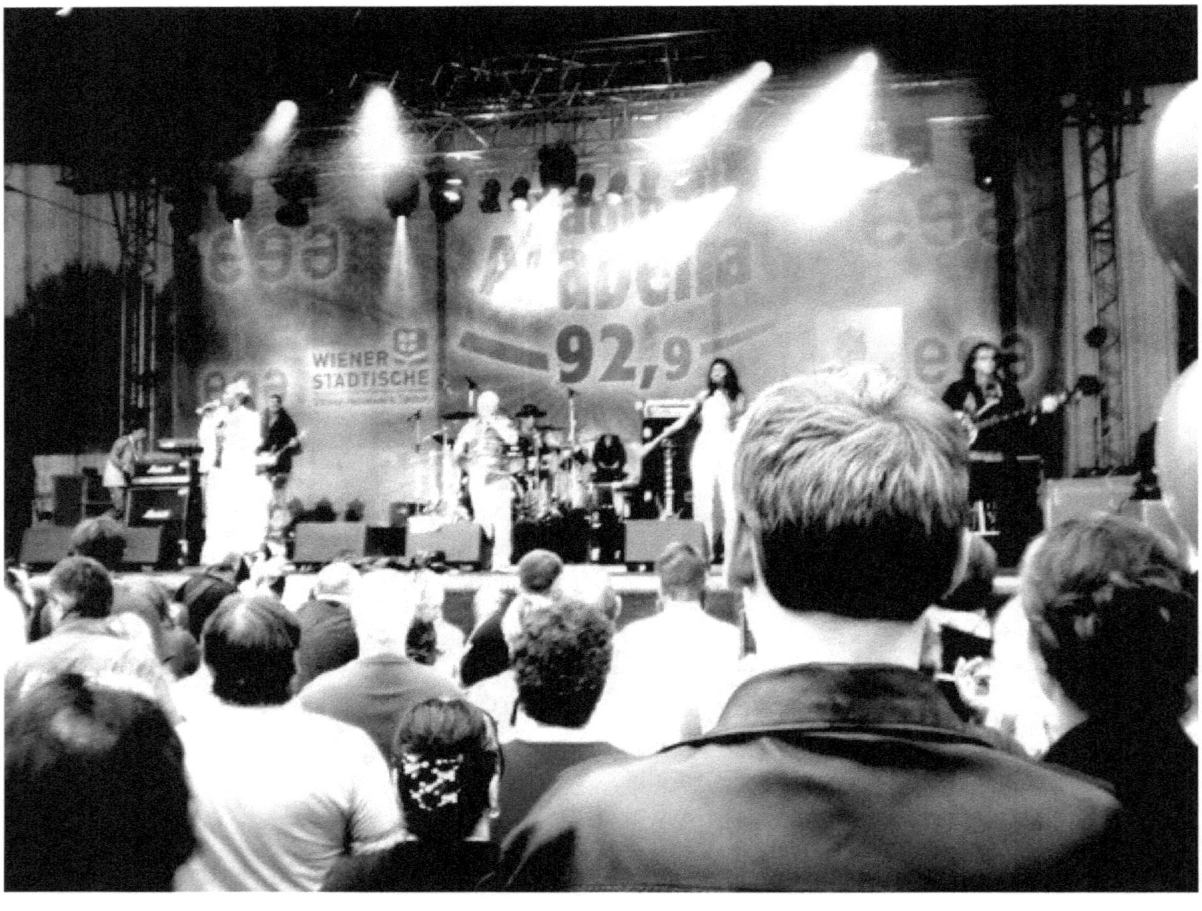
WIENER
STÄDTISCHE
92,9

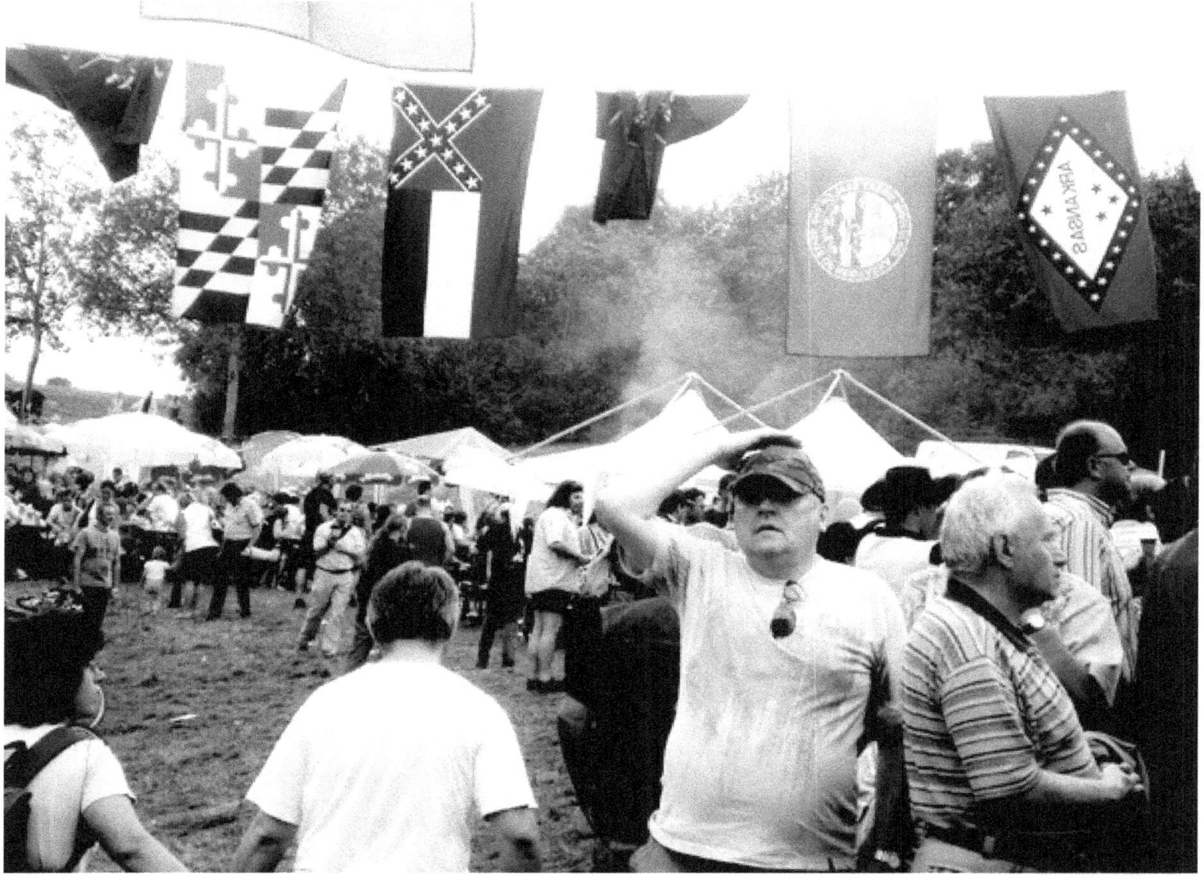

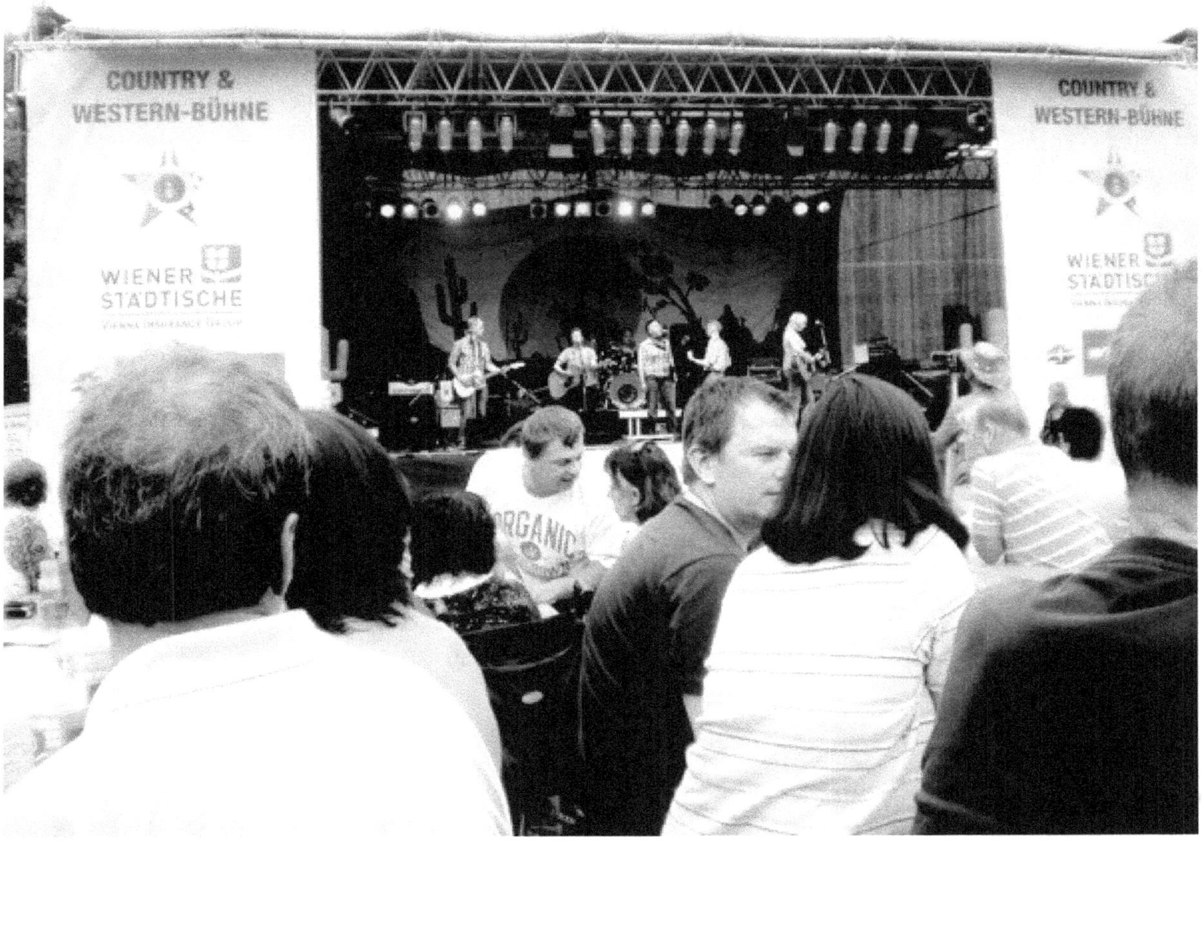
COUNTRY &
WESTERN-BÜHNE
WIENER
STÄDTISCHE
COUNTRY &
WESTERN-BÜHNE
WIENER
STÄDTISCHE
ORGANIC

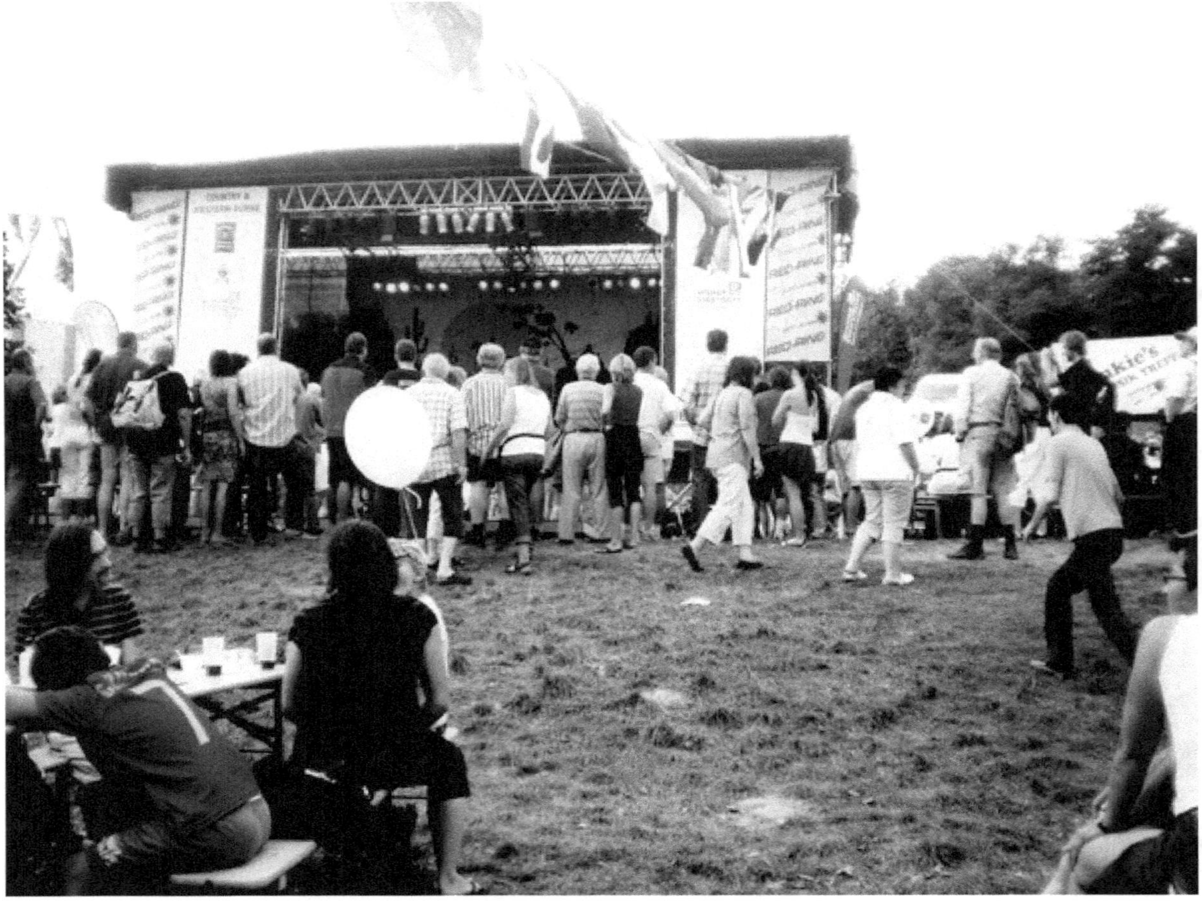

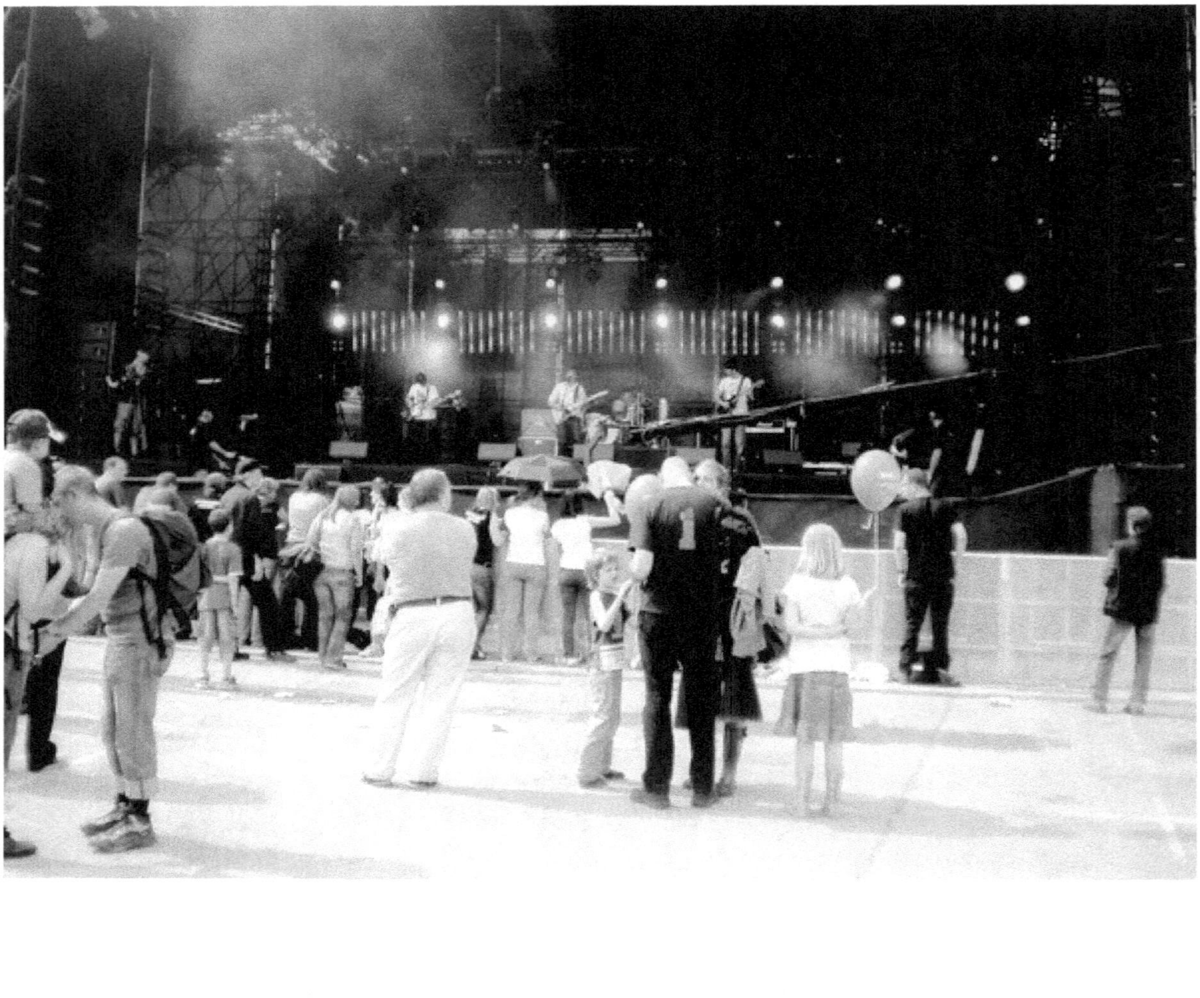

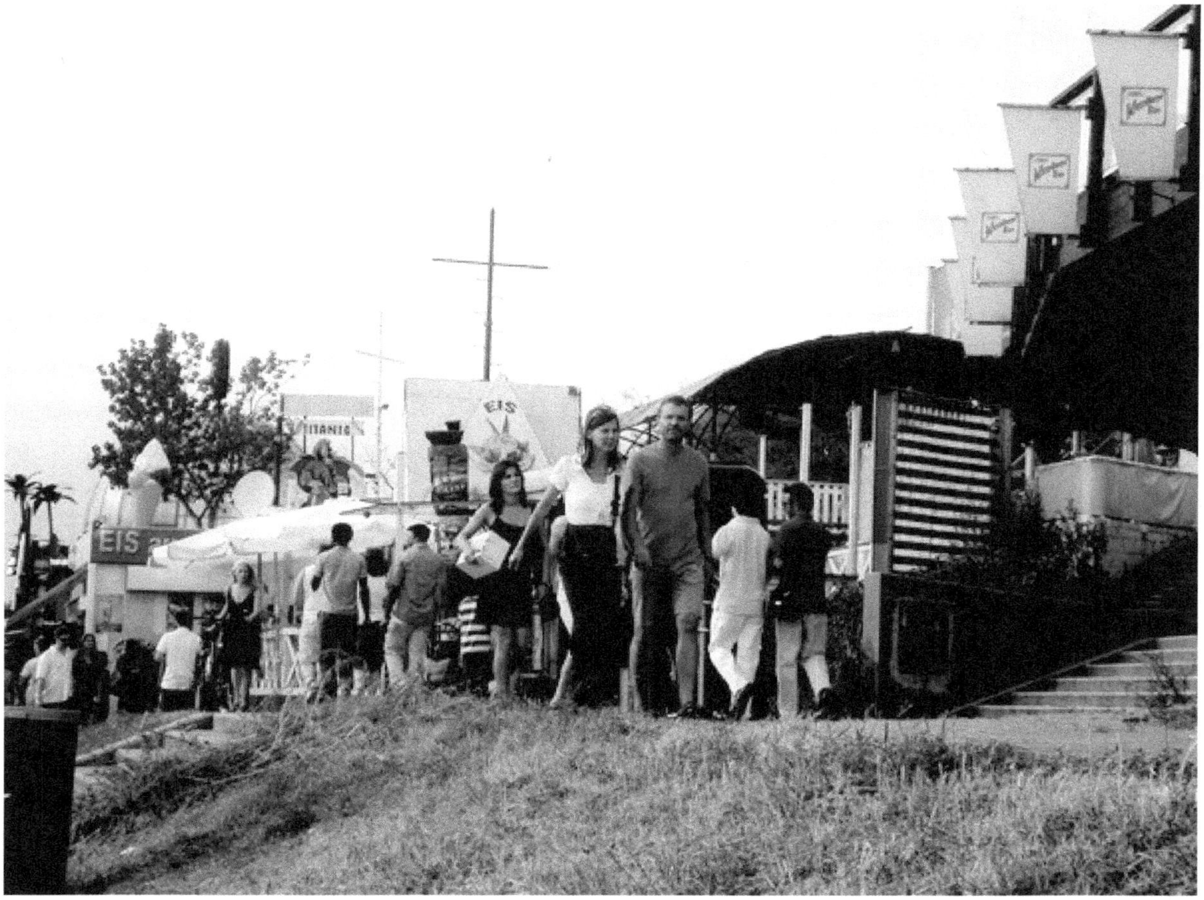
EIS
EIS

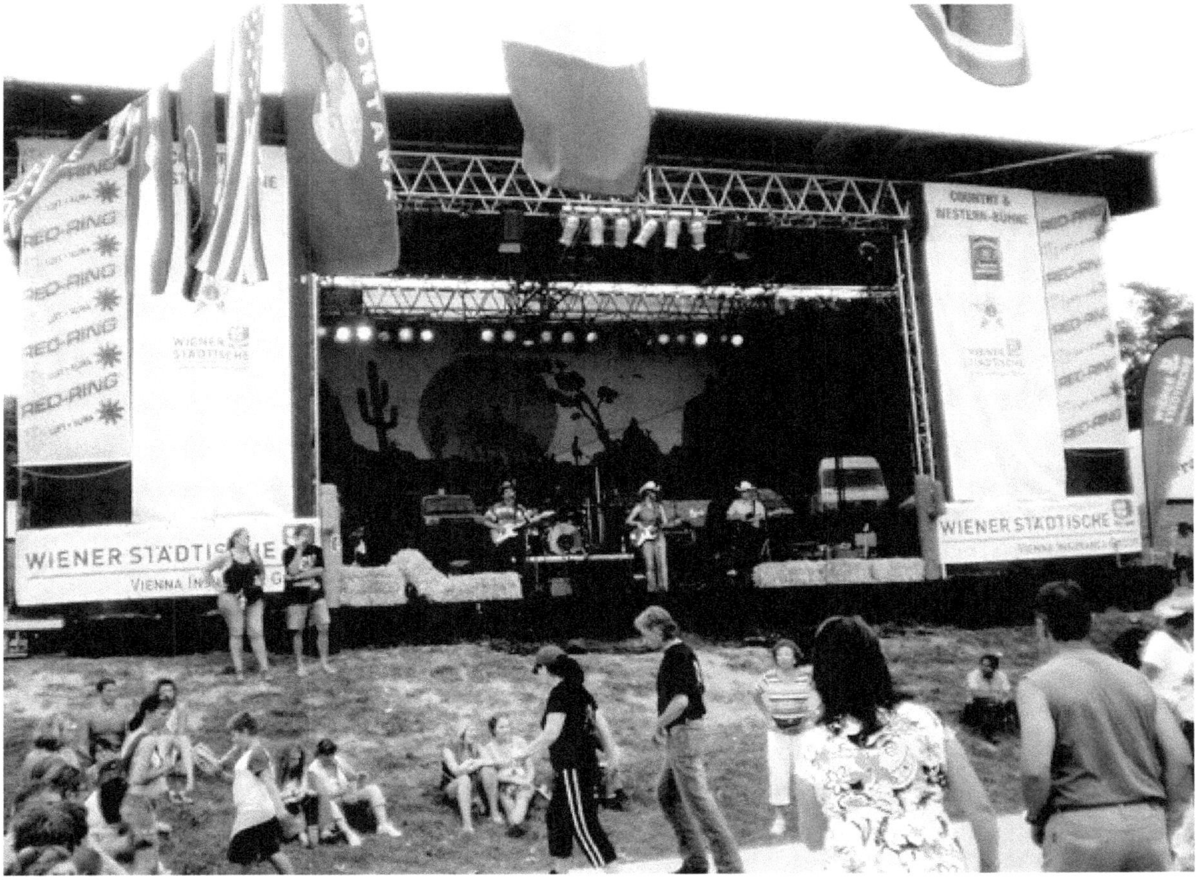
MONTANA
RED-RING
COUNTRY & WESTERN-BÜHNE
WIENER STÄDTISCHE
WIENER STÄDTISCHE

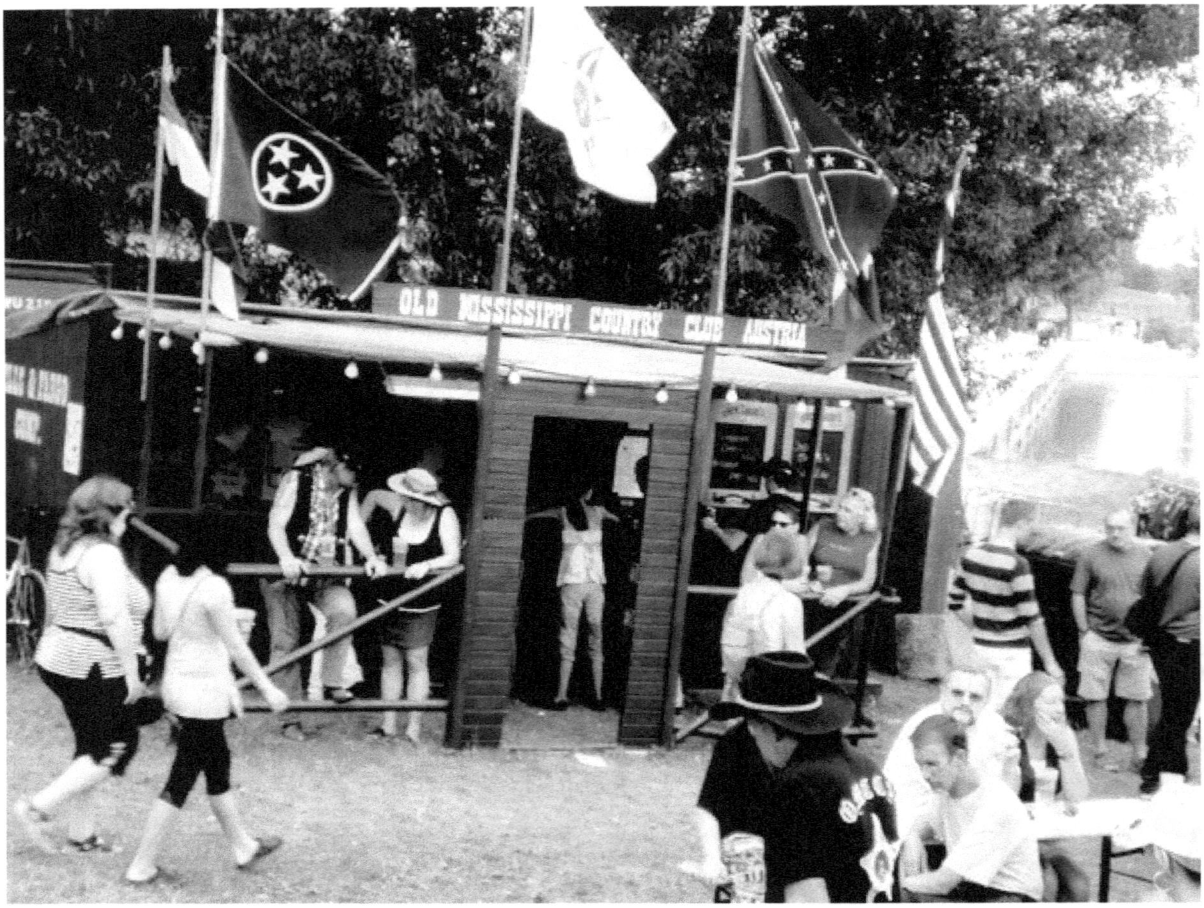
OLD MISSISSIPPI COUNTRY CLUB AUSTRIA

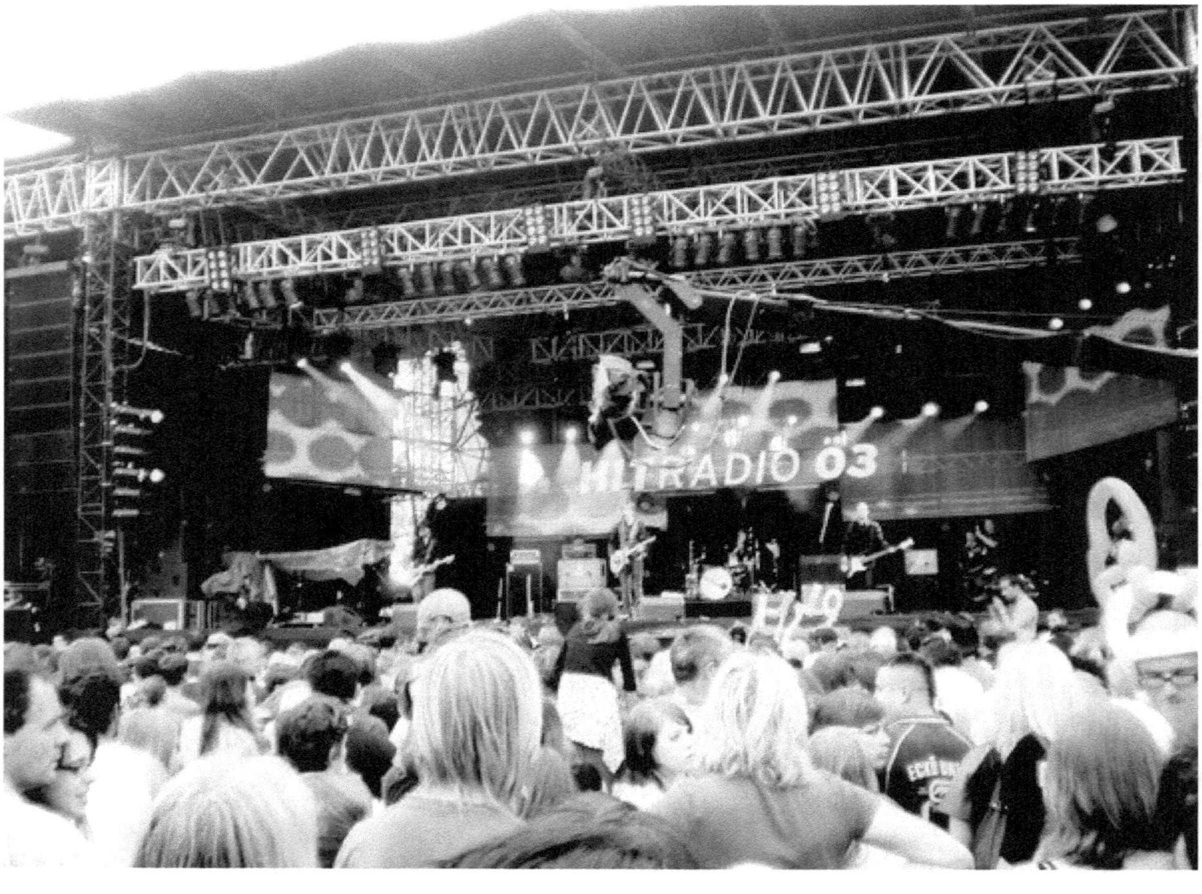
HITRADIO Ö3

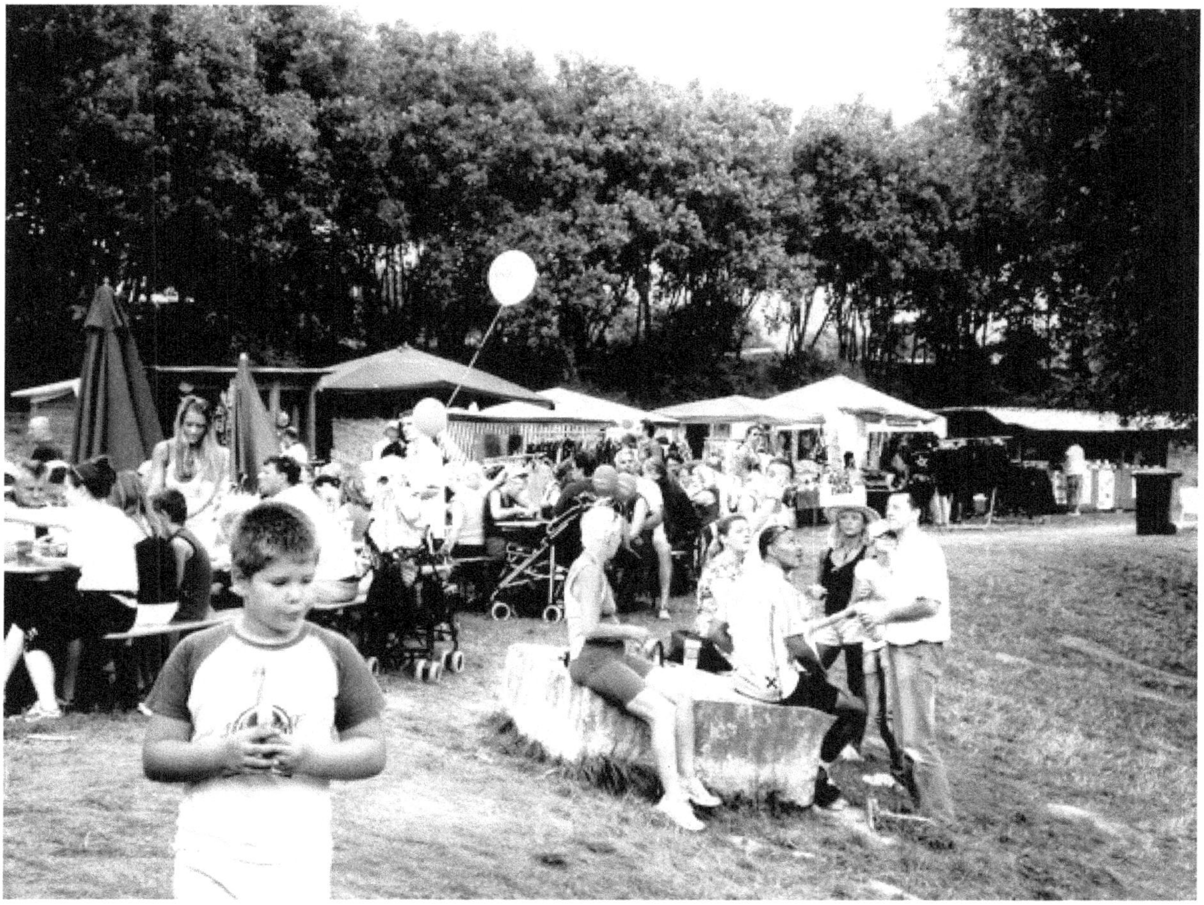

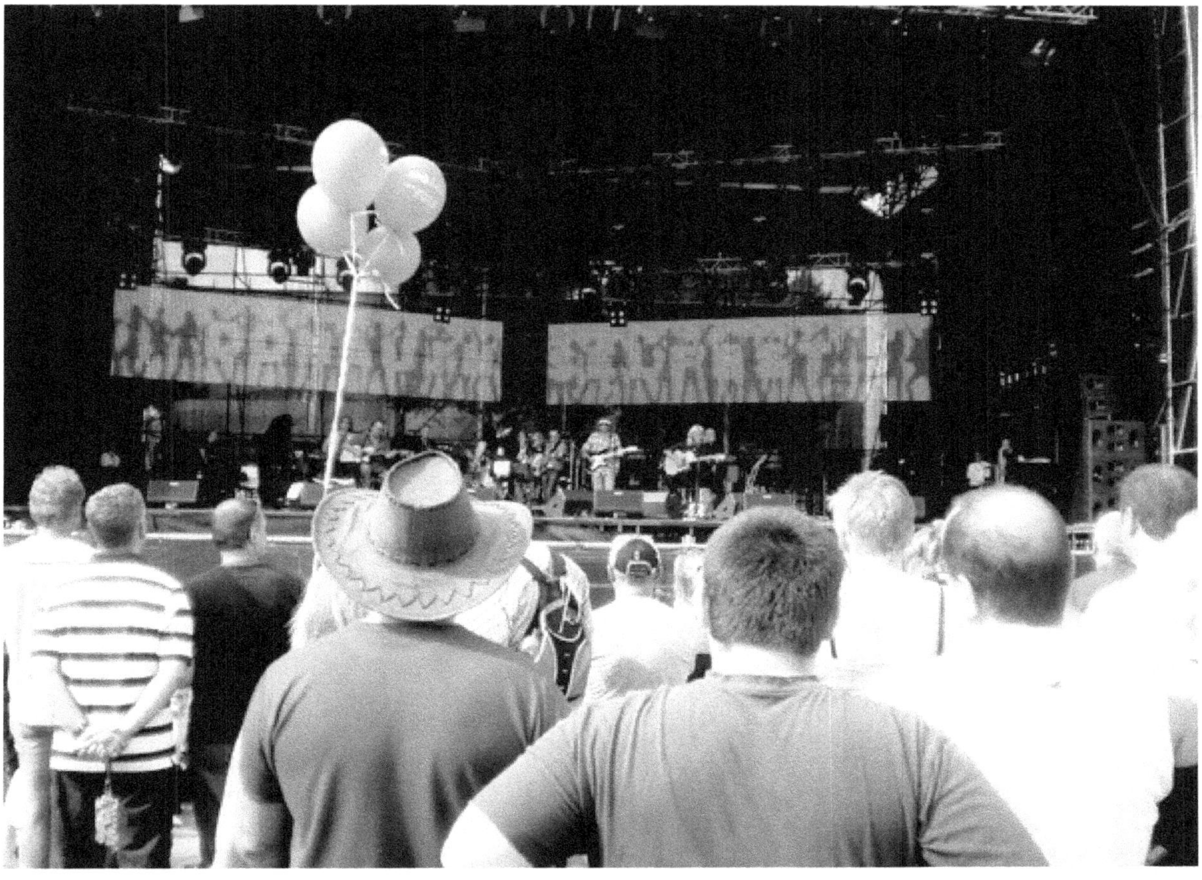

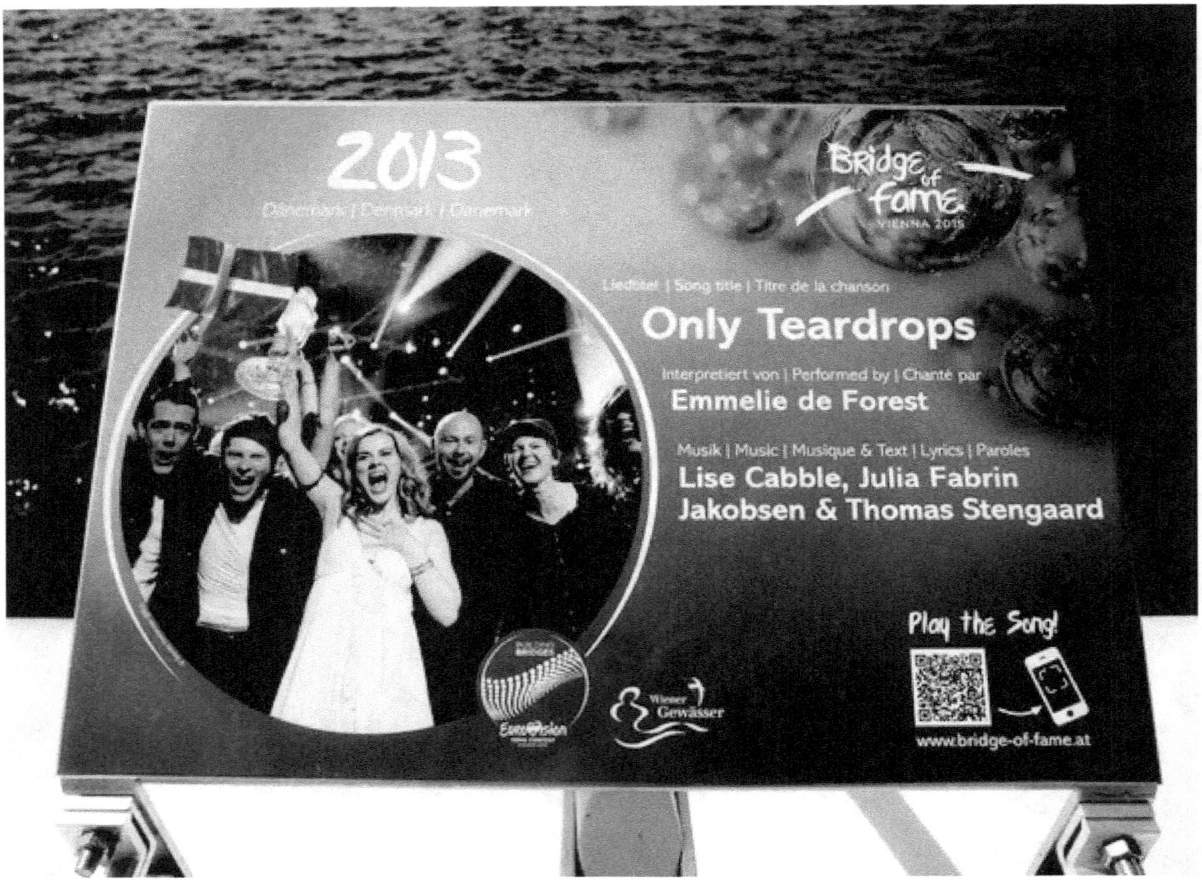
2013
Dänemark | Denmark | Danemark
Bridge of Fame
VIENNA 2015
Liedtitel | Song title | Titre de la chanson
Only Teardrops
Interpretiert von | Performed by | Chanté par
Emmelie de Forest
Musik | Music | Musique & Text | Lyrics | Paroles
Lise Cabble, Julia Fabrin
Jakobsen & Thomas Stengaard
Play the Song!
www.bridge-of-fame.at

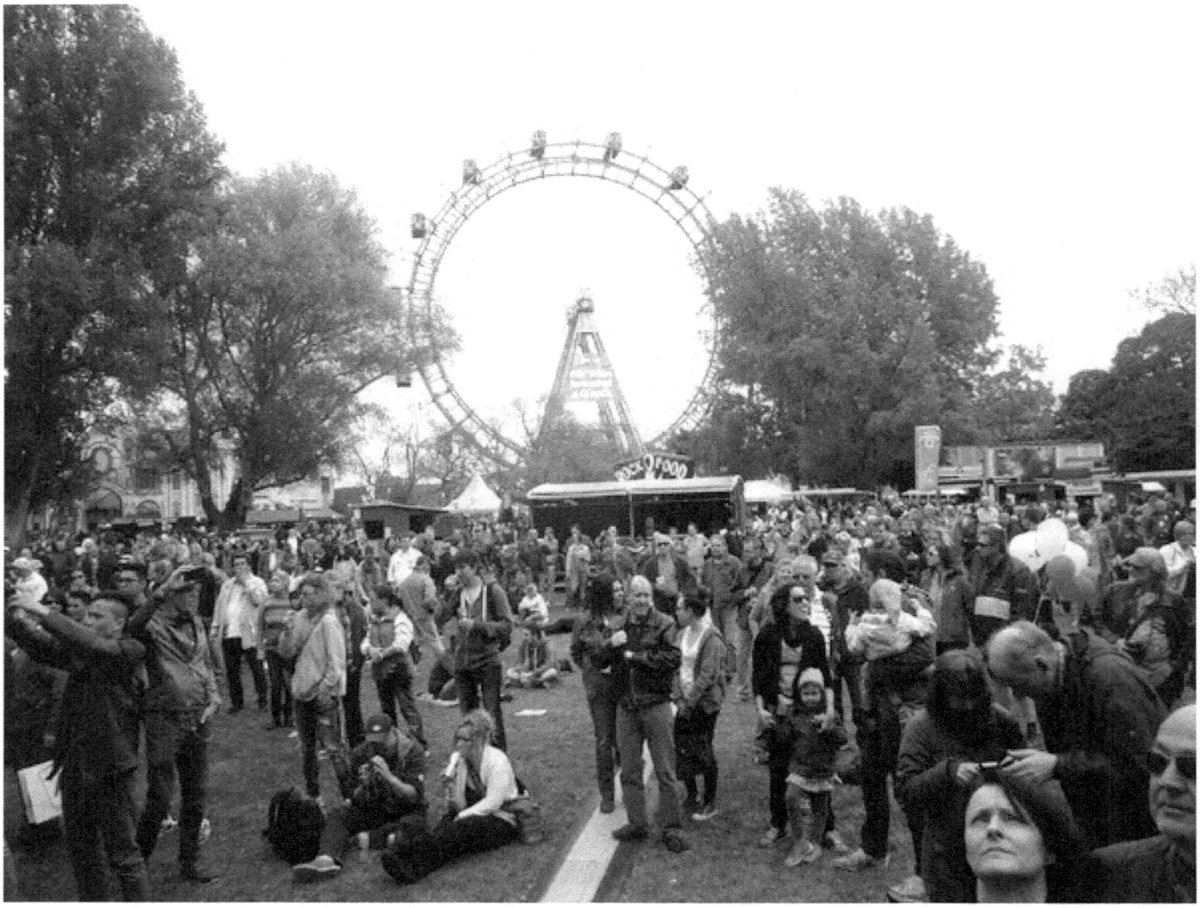

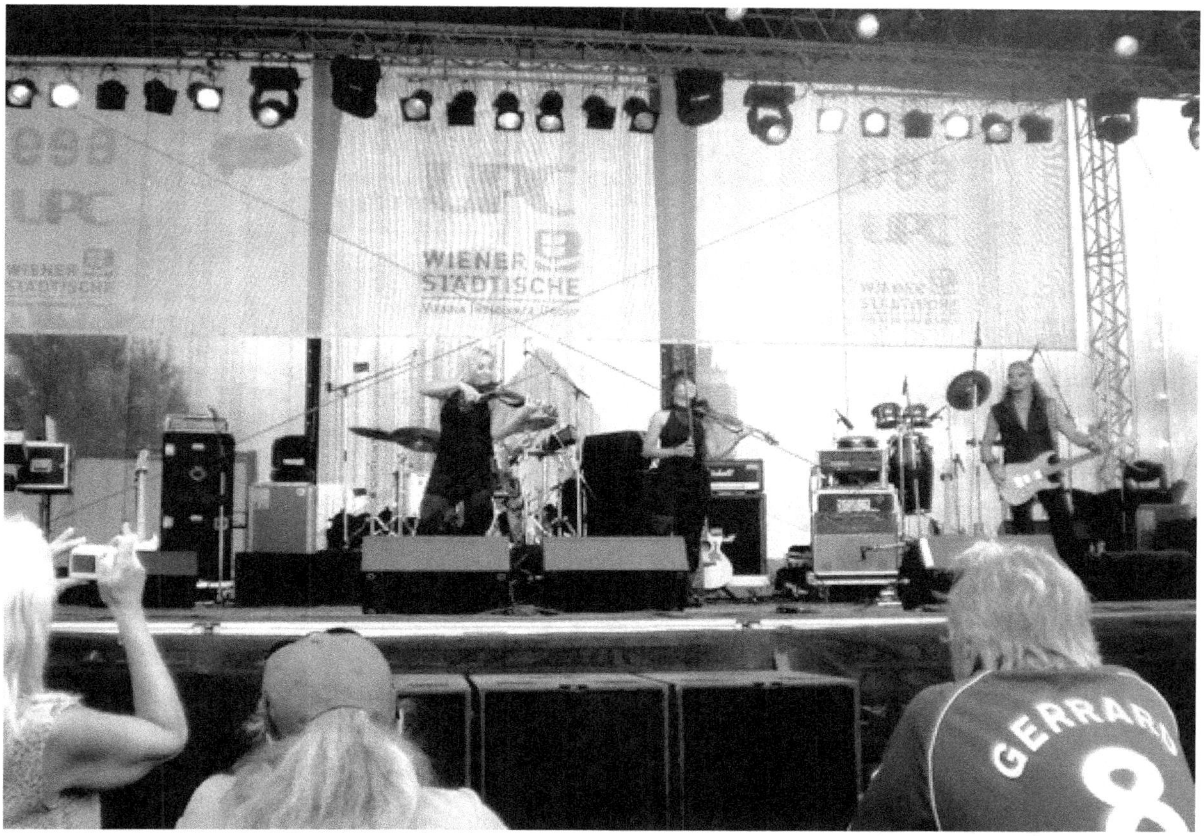
WIENER
STÄDTISCHE
GERRARD
8

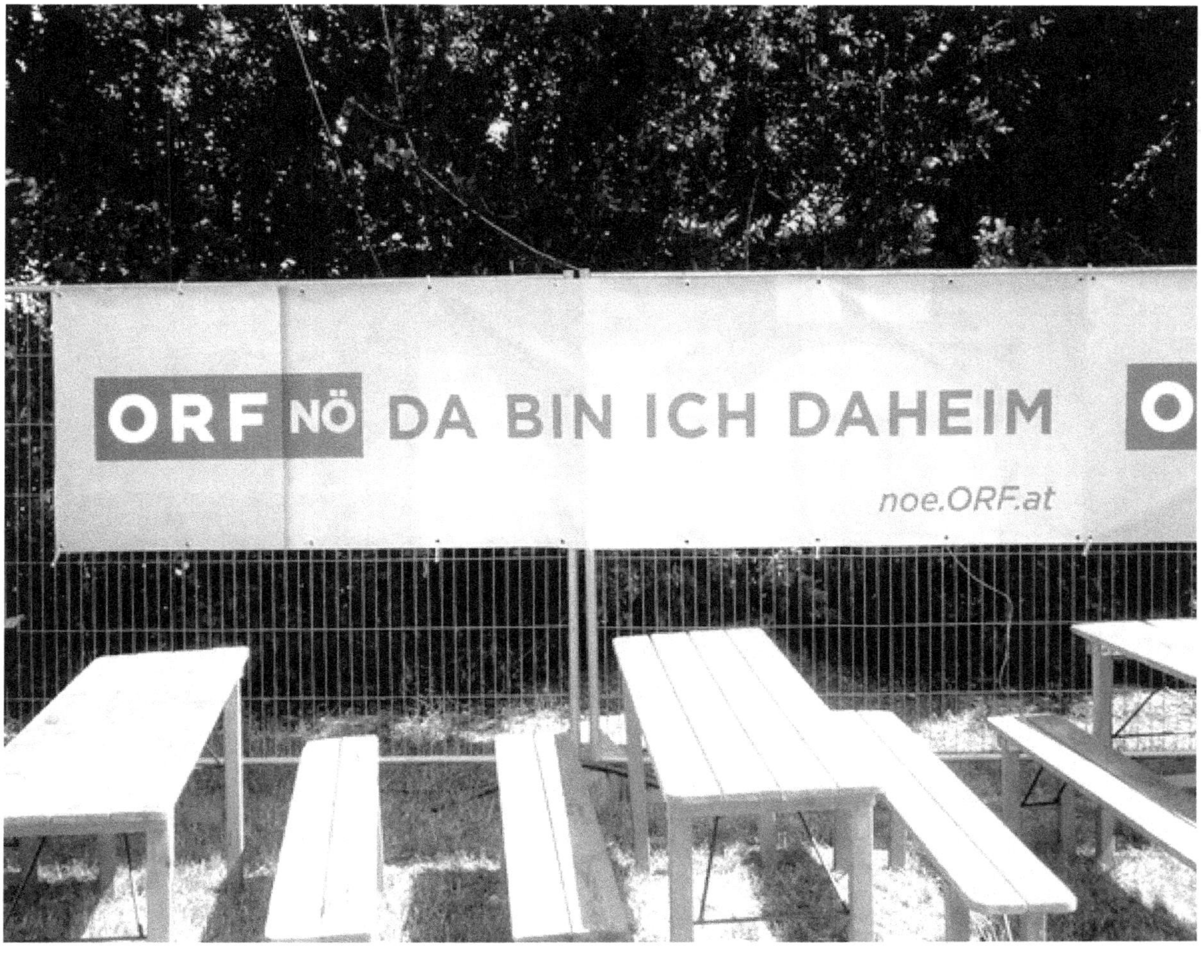
ORF NÖ DA BIN ICH DAHEIM
noe.ORF.at

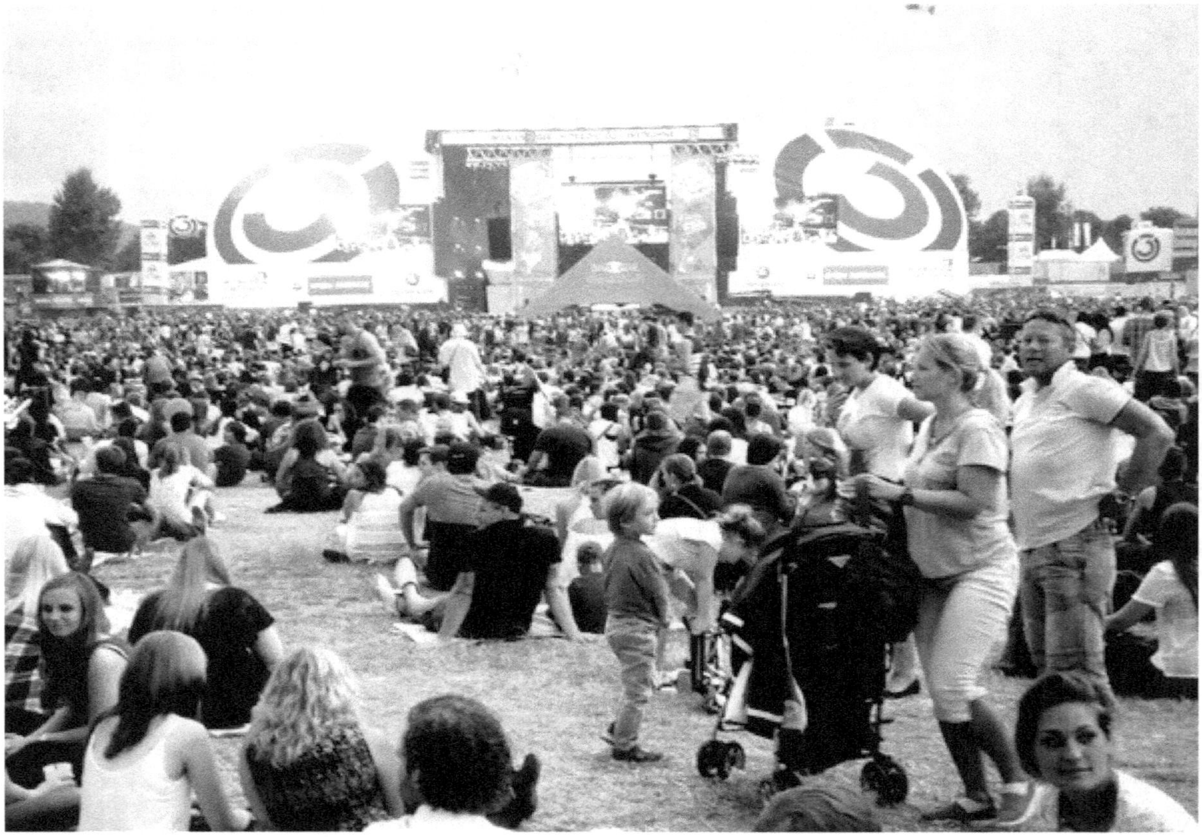

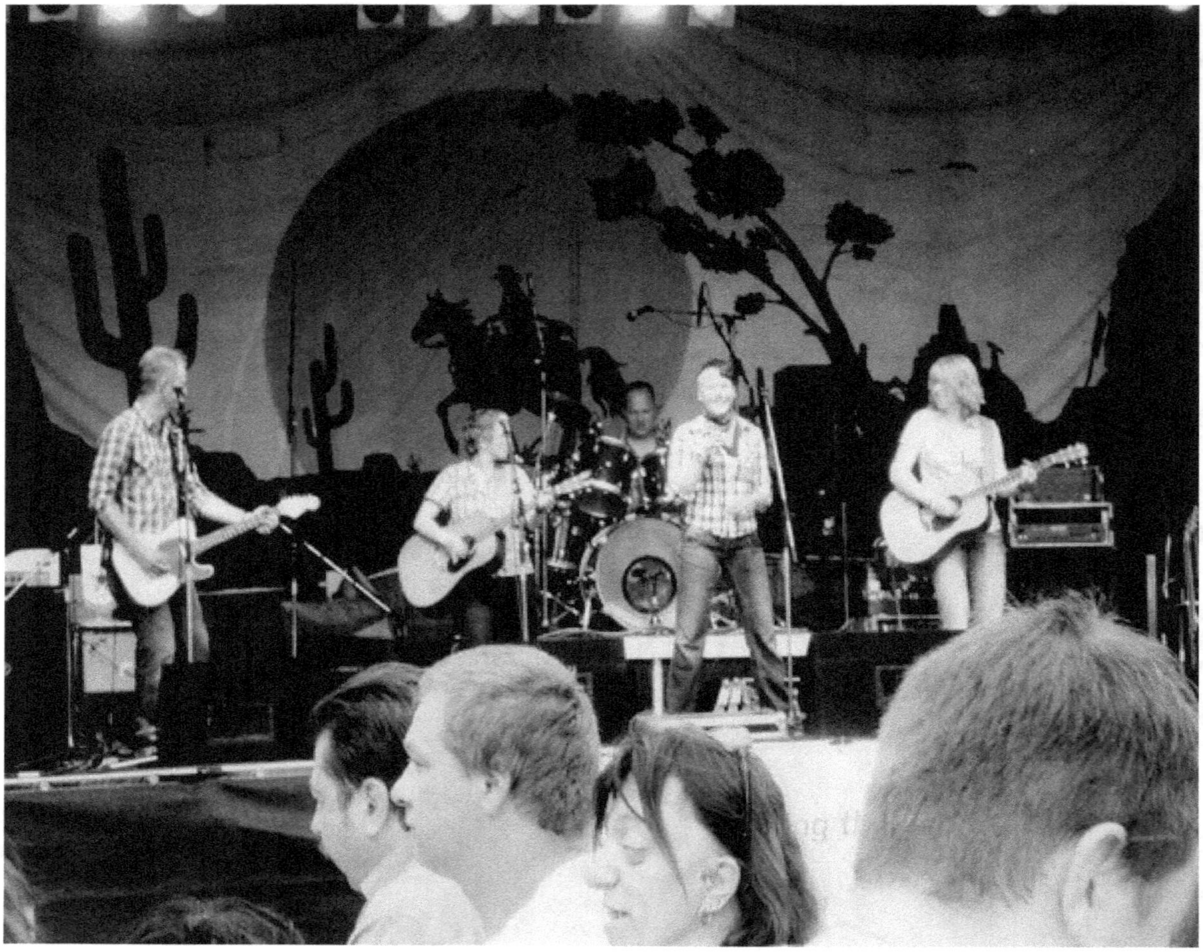

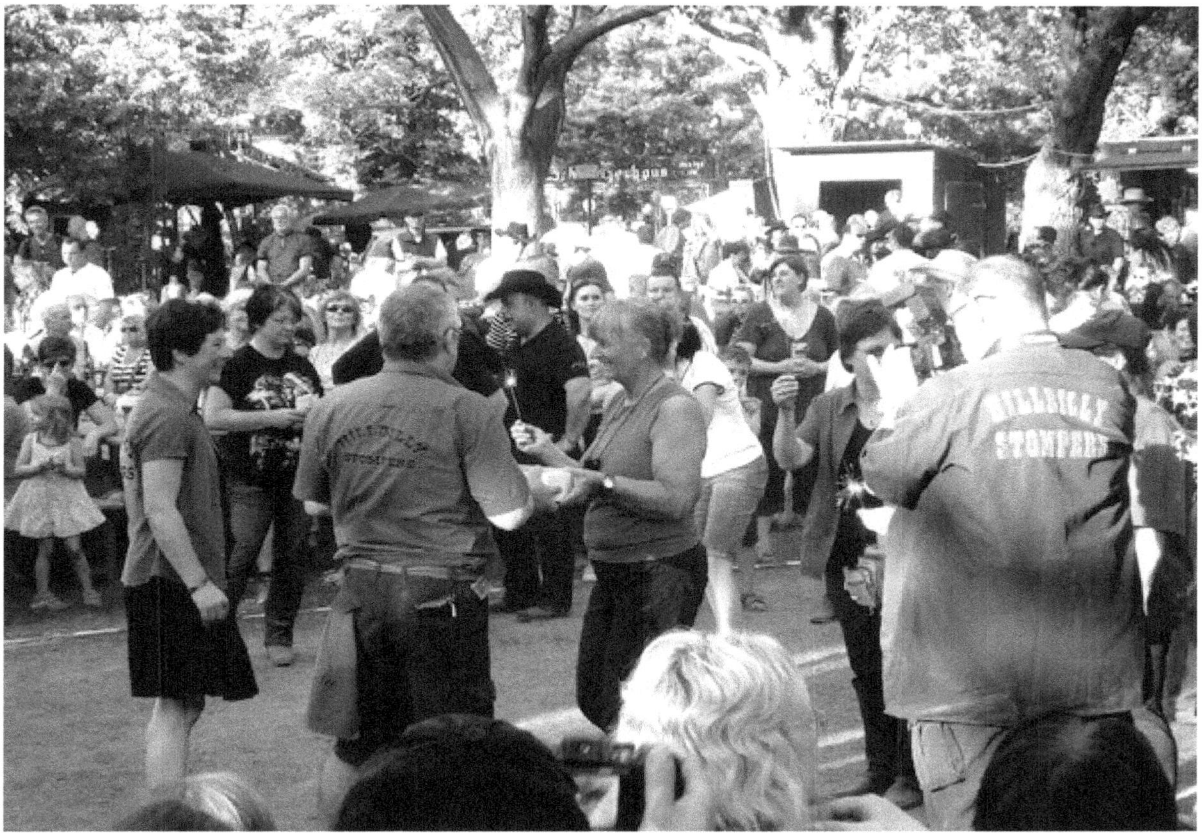

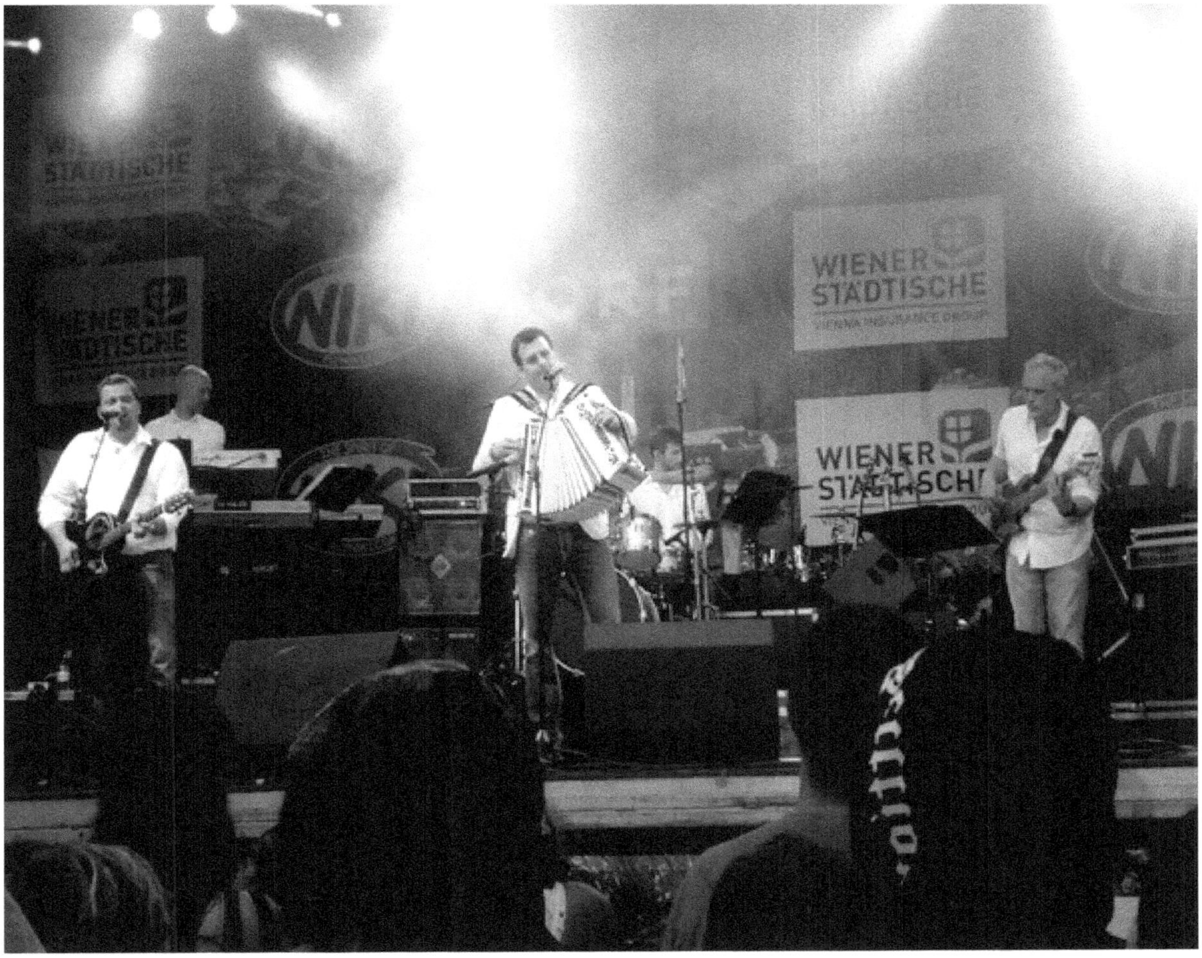
WIENER
STÄDTISCHE

www.ingramcontent.com/pod-product-compliance
Lightning Source LLC
Chambersburg PA
CBHW080606190526
45169CB00007B/2895
* 9 7 8 1 5 3 0 3 7 9 6 4 4 *